TEACHING ENGLISH
WITH
DRAMA

Teaching English with Drama

Also available in the Teaching English series:

Teaching English One to One   ISBN 1-898789-12-3

Teaching English with Drama   ISBN 1-898789-11-6

Teaching English with Information Technology   ISBN 1-898789-16-1

Lessons in Your Rucksack   ISBN 1-898789-14-7

Guide to English Language Teaching   ISBN 1-898789-17-8

For full details of all our books and our range of magazines for teachers and students, including:

     English Teaching Professional

     Modern English Teacher

     Modern English Digest

     ESL Magazine

Visit our website:

www.KeywaysPublishing.com

TEACHING ENGLISH
WITH
DRAMA

Mark Almond

Keyways Publishing

Teaching English With Drama

Published by: **Keyways Publishing Ltd**
PO Box 100, Chichester,
West Sussex, PO18 8HD, UK

First published 2005 by Modern English Publishing Ltd

Tel: +44 (0)1243 576444
Fax: +44 (0)1243 576456
Email: info@keywayspublishing.com
Website: www.KeywaysPublishing.com

British Library Cataloguing-in-Publication Data

A catalogue record for this book is available from the British Library

ISBN 1-898789-11-6

Design by Navigator Guides

Editor Francesca Collin

Layout by MEP

Printed by RPM, Chichester, UK

Contents

Dedication

This book is for Catherine and Harvey.

Thanks

I would like to thank all those students and teachers I have worked with over the years who have supported my belief in the value of drama in language teaching by so enthusiastically taking part in projects and workshops and giving me constructive feedback, all of which has helped shape my approach to using drama in ELT. Here, I include the first students I produced a play with at Stafford House School of English, Canterbury; students at Anglian School of English and Canterbury Christ Church University and teachers on Pilgrims Language Courses and at the Hong Kong institute of Education.

Introduction

My interest in acting goes back to when I was about seven years old. I remember excitedly creating characters and mapping out scenes with my less-than-keen brother, which we would later act out (to nobody) in our back garden. My involvement in stage acting didn't come about until I was 15 and that was purely by accident: a schoolfriend of mine wanted to audition for *Kes*, a play based on Barry Hines's novel set in the north of England about a young, under-privileged boy whose only interest in life, which was to rear a kestrel he had caught himself. I went along to the audition to support my friend, read, and was given the lead role. I have been fascinated by the art of acting ever since.

Of course my initial interest in drama or play-acting at seven years old is nothing unusual amongst children, as Winston and Tandy (2001: vii-viii) observe: "Since we [*people*] were very young children, we have learned to distinguish between the conventions of play and those of everyday life and exploring the boundaries between the two can be a great source of delight … it is from children's innate capacity for play, and upon the understandings they gain from participating in play, that dramatic activity can be constructed". To an extent, we unfortunately tend to lose this playfulness as we get older primarily because we are seldom given the opportunity to *play* in this way: enacting scenes in which people get angry, but nobody *really* gets angry or someone loses their job, but nobody *really* loses their job. Over the years of using drama techniques in my teaching and training, I have witnessed students and teachers alike approach the work with great alacrity because they are being given the opportunity to play (experiment), learn and practise living in the target language in a wholly supportive, unconventional, creative and fun way.

Section One:
Why Use Drama?

Chapter 1

The benefits of acting skills for EFL/ESL learners and teachers

In the 1980s, some ELT writers and drama specialists felt drama needed to be demystified (Wessels, 1987) and proffered that drama was almost impossible to define due to its intangibility and immeasurability (Hayes, 1984). I think most language teachers these days know what drama is and they recognise its value in ELT but, casting an eye over current coursebooks, resource books, supplementary material and teacher training syllabuses, there continues to be a need for a more substantial inclusion of drama. Teachers still need practical guidance on how to incorporate drama more comprehensively and cohesively into their teaching, with a view to either underpinning their whole classroom practice with it or running an extra-curricular drama club after school.

The principal purpose of this book is to provide EFL/ESL teachers (although it is relevant to any language teaching) with an accessible collection of drama activities which form a step-by-step guide to putting on a published play with a group of language learners and it aims to demonstrate how this process accurately targets the requirements of a communicative approach to language teaching. It is designed more with the secondary school or adult learner in mind, although most of the ideas could easily be used or adapted for primary school teaching. This book will also serve those teachers who are not staging a play but would like a broad range of drama activities to supplement their own language or drama teaching as all of the exercises here are easily adaptable.

The Benefits of Acting Skills for Learners

Even though the ideas and exercises here can be adapted and used in isolation to supplement everyday classroom work, I am strongly recommending teachers embrace a drama approach more completely by staging a play with their learners for the following reasons:

- Drama is a whole-person approach to language teaching which requires us to look at communication holistically. Creating a character and acting in a play can be a visceral, intellectual and emotional experience which makes the learning process more meaningful and memorable and more transferable to the real world.

- Acting helps build confidence, because apart from the aspect of performance and the rapturous applause that usually accompanies it, it is totally collaborative and mutually supportive. We rely on each other to succeed in producing something of value and quality.

- The group shares the same objective and putting on a play provides a tangible and achievable target to work towards.

- Working within the framework of a play contextualises all the related language work.

- The process of building a character can make us aware of the needs and character traits of people we come into contact with in our daily lives, which is important in real-life communication and interaction. In mixed-nationality classes, cultural difference are spontaneously revealed, which helps us to understand each other better.

- Putting on a play together as a group trains students in problem solving as constantly throughout the rehearsal period we are faced with decisions that have to be made or hurdles that have to be overcome. These could be of a technical nature (lighting/sound/props etc) or related to the acting. It is invaluable language practice for students to do this kind of collaborating and problem-solving in English.

- Producing a play allows us to explore and develop characters whose lives we only see a small part of on stage. This provides enormous scope for improvising scenes not in the play and generates discussion of the characters' thoughts, words and actions.

- Using an authentic script lends itself well to exploring features such as connected speech, expressing attitude with the voice, intonation patterns and sentence stress. Contemporary plays have a wealth of idiomatic language and samples of speech which reflect how English is used in the real world. Such plays also allow us to study communicative strategies such as hesitation devices, false starts and circumlocution.

- Well-written plays by and large consist of short utterances, again reflecting authentic language use and these are useful in the internalisation and memorisation of vocabulary and functional chunks of language. On several occasions, students have commented that they have used 'chunks' from the play in their everyday lives.
- The only teaching materials required when producing a play are the scripts.
- Being part of this kind of group activity is enormous fun and highly rewarding.

With such high priority now being placed on building our learners' confidence, improving their spontaneity, developing their fluency and generally strengthening their ability to communicate in realistic situations, we need to provide them with 'rehearsals for life'. Drama attempts to bridge the gap between the carefully controlled language work that is often done in the classroom and the complexity of unpredictable language and behaviour we are confronted with in the outside world by physically and emotionally engaging our students in safe and occasionally unsafe situations. It is a whole-person approach in that it doesn't deal exclusively with spoken language but rather requires our learners to react and respond with their intellects, emotions and natural instincts. Drama also examines and practises these broader aspects of communication:

- gesture and gesticulation;
- facial expression;
- eye contact and eye movement;
- posture and movement;
- proxemics;
- prosody (pitch, tone, volume, tempo).

This book is not suggesting we should be training our learners to become accomplished actors but rather it demonstrates how we can learn from the process many professional actors follow to create a character and ultimately a piece of theatre and how this type of work can be applied to a communicative language learning situation. There is the element of performance or end product which brings its own benefits, but the emphasis is much more on the process and on how all language skill development can be integrated when using a script using your *self* as your main source of reference.

The Benefits of Acting Skills for Teachers

Admittedly this does not directly relate to the subject of this book but because it is essential for all teachers to be able to stimulate and maintain the interest of their students and make genuine communication with them, this short section has been included to illustrate the common ground shared by teachers and actors.

There is clearly far more to teaching than just possessing subject knowledge. On a daily basis as teachers, we have to communicate and interact with our students and transmit our knowledge to them in an entertaining and memorable way. It is our job to create the most appropriate environment for learning to take place. We have to deal with a room full of human beings, all with their own individual needs and preferred learning styles, not to mention the different emotions they may be feeling at the time they enter the room. Occasionally, we have to cope with students who would much rather be elsewhere. Furthermore, as teachers, we often have to improvise and make spontaneous decisions if, for example, the lesson starts to drag or go in an unexpected direction or if we are asked an unexpected question. It is, therefore, useful and apposite to evaluate certain skills actors possess and ascertain to what extent they can be applied to the art of teaching.

The obvious connection between teacher and actor is that both have an 'audience' to which ideas, feelings and knowledge must be transmitted in a captivating, entertaining and memorable way. The ideas below are applicable to the teaching of any subject but are in some ways particularly pertinent to drama and producing a play in that teachers should, whenever possible, lead by example. It is recommended they actually do the warm-up exercises themselves with their students and, if necessary, perform a section of text to clarify to a learner how it *could* be done. In drama, it is important for students to witness teachers participating in activities to reassure them that what we are asking them to do is not an unreasonable or impossible request and we are willing to risk making ourselves look silly too.

David Raven once held the world record for being 'the most durable actor' due to his 4,575 appearances as Major Metcalf in *The Mousetrap* in London's West End. Theatre actors are often in long-running plays and have to keep their performances as fresh as the first time they play the character. Each time actors utter their lines, it should be as though it is for the first time in their character's life. In order for teachers to captivate and hold the interest of their students, they too need to adopt similar enthusiasm, energy and freshness. It is essential that teachers' material is second nature to them so that it can be delivered naturally and energetically so that they can communicate the content as themselves.

According to Tauber and Mester, we can convey enthusiasm with:
- voice and body animation;
- classroom space;
- humour.

(*Tauber and Mester, 1994:14*)

Teachers and actors need to be aware of and sensitised to their own voices, gestures, facial expressions and movement. As teachers, we would do well to constantly question the impact our voices, facial expressions and body language have on our students because we cannot *not* communicate – our faces, bodies and voices always convey some message to our listeners but unfortunately, we are not always aware of what that message might be.

Voice and Body

The key to an effective use of voice and body in the classroom is variety but of course learners will only respond positively if the 'animation' is *natural*: "Like actors, teachers should act with a *moderate* level of animation, as is appropriate to their own enjoyment of the subject matter and of the process of teaching and learning" (*ibid, 1994: 32*).

Non-excessive movement of the body, including facial expression and eye contact, is especially linked to the effective teaching of language because gesture and facial expression help clarify and demonstrate meaning and above all are expressive and can supplement the verbal message. Making *genuine* eye contact with students is equally important because it makes a connection between speaker and listener and narrows the distance between them, thereby helping maintain the interest and attention of learners.

At this point, I would encourage you to look at the exercises in the Vocal Warm-up chapter (*Chapter 5, p.64 onwards*) and decide which ones are applicable to teaching, e.g. Exercise 11, Poetry Alive! because it deals quite exhaustively with breathing, volume, pace, pitch and tone, all of which "contribute to a teacher's perceived credibility and control of the classroom situation, thus enhancing learning in the long term" (*ibid, 1994: 49*), and quite simply, learners are more likely to remain attentive and responsive to a more animated rather than monotonous voice. As Maley explains: "The voice is a teacher's most frequently-used and important teaching aid … but teachers continue to take their most precious asset, their voice, for granted" (*Maley, 2000: vii*). As well as participating fully with students in vocal warm-ups in a drama lesson, it is also recommended that teachers spend just fifteen minutes each day on voice exercises to promote relaxation, increase range and resonance, release the voice and become aware of its emotive power.

Movement and Space

In theatre, determining where an actor moves or stands on stage is called 'blocking'. This is mapped out in detail during the rehearsal period and usually leaves little room for deviation. Blocking is vital in establishing relationships between characters, maintaining audience interest and controlling audience attention. In the same way, teachers should vary the way space is used in the classroom and how different seating arrangements can help maintain interest and motivation during the lesson. The layouts probably most conducive to whole-class drama work (not including running through the play) are with chairs only in a horseshoe shape or a complete circle. In small groupwork, if you have the space and moveable furniture, you can cluster chairs around the entire space. All of these configurations ensure maximum visibility between learners and the teacher and allow adequate space for all to move around in.

In a conventional classroom in a non-drama lesson, this might not be physically possible or desired but just as actors make effective and meaningful use of space on stage, so too can teachers vary *their* position in the classroom, which is clearly much easier than trying to reconfigure the entire room. Consider the effect the following might have on the dynamics and focus of a lesson when the teacher changes his/her proximity to the learners:

- teaching from the back of the classroom making the back-row students the front-row students and vice versa;
- kneeling or crouching down between desks;
- crouching down at the front of the room;
- sitting behind a vacant desk amongst the students;
- sitting on the teacher's desk;
- sitting on a student's desk;
- sitting on the floor;
- leaning on a student's desk entering his/her personal space;
- weaving slowly between the students' desks;
- standing in the doorway;
- standing on a chair or table.

Some of these are extreme and you may never consider trying them out but what is clear is that creative use of space can help establish the desired relationship between teacher and learners and it can maintain attentiveness and responsiveness by varying the focus and in some cases hierarchy, for example when the teacher sits in a vacant student's chair rather than at the front of the class which makes him/her appear 'in charge'.

Humour

There are some important reasons why humour should judicially be incorporated into any lesson. Humour:

- can help the teacher be viewed more positively by students;
- conveys enthusiasm;
- acts as an effective mnemonic device;
- reduces anxiety and tension;
- can maintain student attention.

The above points all lead to increased motivation and deepen the relationship between learners and the teacher. As with creative use of voice, body animation and space, humour should be used in moderation and teachers should avoid making too many self-deprecating remarks and remarks that will lower the self-esteem of the learners just to get a laugh. It also goes without saying that most kinds of humour ie. those which show the more vulnerable side to human nature, should only be used if there is trust between all those concerned and the relationship between the teacher and students is healthy. Below are ways in which I have tried to inject humour into my classes, some of which you might think are a little risky but I have never used them to blatantly deride or patronise students – rather to gently cajole them into producing language, a correct answer or pronunciation – and it has always been received in the manner it was intended:

- making strange (but encouraging!) noises and contorting my face to steer a learner to a correct answer or pronunciation (sharp intakes of breath and tight eyes work well);
- wiping my brow accompanied by an audible 'phew' followed by a "Well done"! when a student has struggled and succeeded in producing a response;
- feigning a heart attack and contorting my face in agony if a student is *so close* to getting the right answer or producing a piece of 'correct' English;
- pretending to faint and giving lots of praise if a student is contributing well during a class or has answered a difficult question;
- if I make a spelling mistake on the board, I blame the pen;
- if I ask a student a question and s/he doesn't know the answer or is taking a long time to formulate the answer, I say "Thank you" – as if s/he *has* answered;
- if a student is taking an extremely long time to formulate an answer, I start snoring in an exaggerated way. Only try this with students who you know can take a joke and will not take offence;
- if a story or joke flops, I remind the class that I will be writing their reports at the end of term – laughter usually follows;
- if I'm going to use a picture or a prop later on in the lesson, I display it immediately at the beginning in order to arouse my students' curiosity;
- when drawing a picture on the board, I point out that this is the reason I became a language teacher and not an art teacher;

- I use vocal sound effects to denote punctuation e.g. a quacking noise for a comma and a popping sound for a full stop. This is particularly useful when practising structures such as conditionals or relative clauses;
- if the pronunciation of –ed at the end of a regular verb should be /t/ and I get a student to pronounce it in this way, I wipe my eye making out s/he spat in it. I simultaneously praise the student's contribution;
- holding up two fingers if a learner's sentence requires the preposition 'to' and four fingers if it requires 'for'.

In this short section, my intention is not to suggest we should become hammy, wildly-gesticulating stand-up comedians to get our students' attention but it seems clear that using certain dramaturgical devices in moderation can increase motivation, enhance classroom dynamics and improve student-student and student-teacher relationships, all of which undoubtedly contribute to better learning.

Chapter 2

The Play: a step-by-step guide, from choosing to performing

Criteria for choosing a play for performance

Before embarking on a production, it is essential you choose your play carefully as you and your learners will be working with it quite intensively and over a relatively long period. It is hoped that your choice will take most if not all of the following criteria into account:

- Use a one-act play. They usually last for a maximum of 45 minutes, which is manageable for most EFL/ESL students.
- At higher levels especially, avoid plays specially written for ELT. They are often contrived and lack the natural use of idiom and features of spoken discourse such as ellipsis, unfinished utterances and interruptions, which are a considerably more accurate reflection of real-world English and which higher level students should be able to cope with. However, this does not preclude the use of 'authentic' plays with low levels as suitable examples do exist, but clearly the choice is more limited.
- The more contemporary the play, the better. As a key objective for using drama in ELT is to bridge the gap between the classroom and the outside world, it is important the play is written in contemporary English with samples of up-to-date idiomatic usage. As a general rule, avoid plays written before the 1960s and plays written in a specific dialect.
- The theme(s) of the play should not be too obscure, the plot should be relatively straightforward and the characters quite easy to relate to.

- Choose a play which doesn't have too many long monologues because it is not advisable to put the burden on individuals – it is, after all, a group project. Therefore, choose a play which has mainly short utterances and is interactive.

- "One cannot expect students to be natural actors and the teacher needs to be sensitive to the group's capability when making the selection" (*Dougill, 1987: 87*). Certainly we must not lose sight of the fact that first and foremost, the production of the play should be for the benefit of the participants but there should always be the desire to produce something to be proud of. Even though your audience, probably consisting of teachers, fellow students and parents will not pay to see the play, your 'actors' will want to offer something of quality. In addition, if sufficient time is spent warming up and improving the dynamics amongst the group, they will feel relaxed and less anxious which automatically leads to their acting more naturally and convincingly.

- Choose a play which isn't too technically complex and doesn't rely on special sound and lighting effects.

Tip Box

- It is possible to put on a one-act play at the end of a nine or ten-week term with two hours of rehearsal per week.
- Give students a copy of the play as soon as possible so they can read it and familiarise themselves with the plot, characters and vocabulary straight away.
- Naturalistic and realistic contemporary plays tend to reflect real-world language more accurately with up-to-date idiomatic expressions and shorter utterances
- Search the internet for a script or order scripts through Samuel French's *The Guide to Selecting Plays*, which has hundreds of choices (www.samuelfrench-london.co.uk)

Suggested Plays

These are examples of plays I have successfully produced with EFL/ESL students:

Ernie's Incredible Illucinations by Alan Ayckbourn;

Us and Them by David Campton;

Post Mortem by Roald Dahl (adapted);

Romeo and Juliet by William Shakespeare (modernised version);

Dreamjobs by Graham Jones;

The Animal Connection by Margaret Bower;

Blah Blah Blah by Brian Marshall;

A Night Out by Harold Pinter.

It is strongly advised you buy a copy of Samuel French's *The Guide to Selecting Plays* (www.samuelfrench-london.co.uk or from 52 Fitzroy Street, London, W1P 6JR). This catalogue probably contains the widest choice of plays available and is usefully put into categories such as Revue Sketches, One Act Plays, Mini Dramas and One Act Plays for Children and Young People.

Casting

How you cast your play depends on when and how you intend holding rehearsals. If you are going to integrate the project into the general syllabus and produce a play with an entire class, let's say with 25 students during normal lesson time, it shouldn't be too difficult finding an appropriate play that caters for that number and/or gender mix: the most comprehensive catalogue of plays I know is Samuel French (www.samuelfrench-london.co.uk) which lists hundreds of plays under sections such as one-act plays and plays for children and young people. Under each listing, there is a brief synopsis, the number of characters in the play and their gender. If you find a play that you would really like to do but don't have the exact number of students or right gender mix for, the following strategies should help:

- **If you don't have enough students of a particular gender:** There are nearly always characters in plays who could be either sex. For example, when I directed A Night Out by Harold Pinter, I simply made the 'barman' a 'barmaid'! Other rôles found in many plays such as teacher, doctor or bank manager that are written with a specific gender in mind can usually quite easily be modified to suit the gender of your student by changing some of the lines. I would recommend you change the sex of the character rather than, for example, make a female student play a man

- **If you have more students than characters:** Recruit some learners (particularly those who aren't keen to act) to be: Stage Manager, who oversees all that goes on backstage (this responsibility could easily be shared by two or even three students); Co-director with you; Assistant Stage Manager, whose vital job it is to note down any blocking that is determined during rehearsal; the person in charge of Sound and Lighting; prompt; someone who helps students learn their lines and backstage crew, who are in charge of scene changes, making sure actors have their props and that the necessary props are on stage

  There are occasionally characters that have very few lines or no lines at all and these can often be either left out altogether or his/her lines can be subsumed into another character's lines

- **If you have more characters than students:** Actors can 'double up' ie. play more than one character.

Perhaps the ideal scenario is if you run an extra-curricular drama club on a voluntary basis. The obvious advantage of this approach is that if students are volunteers, they are more likely to commit themselves fully to the play. If you have time for an audition, the best approach is to arrange an initial short meeting to note the balance of gender, language level and interests of the group and then to look for a suitable play. It is also important at this initial meeting to emphasise the commitment required by the participants but also the wealth of benefits participating in a project of this kind can bring.

I usually hold an audition the following week after I have found a suitable play. It is enormously helpful if the interested students can read the play before the audition as some may become interested in particular characters and it is helpful if they are already familiar with the plot. At this session, we read the entire play through once while I ask broad comprehension questions and where appropriate, I ask individuals to read for more than one character. As well as judging them on their audition, I take into account if someone expresses interest in a particular character and I also use my own knowledge of students to cast and take into account if a student looks right for a part.

> **Tip Box**
>
> - At the very first meeting/rehearsal, emphasise the element of fun as well as the enormous achievement of acting in a play in another language.
> - If it's too time-consuming to hold an audition, simply cast the play yourself going on what you know about the students' personalities as well as their physical appearance. Some students might only want a small part with a few lines or alternatively, some might be keen to take on larger roles. This makes the selection process much easier.

Learning Lines

Strongly encourage students to learn their lines as soon as possible because it can be quite restricting trying to act and hold a book at the same time and you are also restricted with the amount of directing you can do. It is a very liberating feeling when you come off the book!

> **Tip Box**
>
> - Probably the most effective way of learning lines is through old-fashioned repetition so maximise the amount of times you run through scenes at rehearsal so students have to repeat their lines in context and while acting simultaneously.
> - As students often know each other's lines, encourage them to keep the scene running by turning their co-actor's line round so their character can say it.
> - Ask a student who isn't in the scene you're rehearsing to prompt. Prompts should be loud and clear, even during a performance. Insist that only one person prompts.
> - Have quick line run-throughs before rehearsing a scene. This is especially useful in the last third of the rehearsal period.

Probably the most effective way of learning lines is during rehearsal because you are saying the lines and carrying out the corresponding actions simultaneously. Although we should encourage students to be as word-perfect as possible because our co-actors have to pick up their cues and the prompt (if you choose to have one) has to follow the dialogue, I tend not to be too strict if books are down and occasionally actors have to paraphrase. In fact, it shows great spontaneity and confidence if a student can ad lib. On the next page is a list of suggestions on line-learning you might like to present to your students:

Tips for Learning Lines

1. Encourage students to pair up with a 'line-learning buddy' who they get together with as often as possible to test each other on their lines.

2. If you have a long speech, read the first line and memorise it by saying it back to yourself. Then read and memorise the first and second lines and say both lines back to yourself. Continue doing this until you get to the end of the speech. This is a very effective method because you gradually build up the speech rather than try to learn all the lines in one chunk.

3. Record yourself reading the scenes in which you appear, including your own lines. As you listen back to it, say your lines over the recording. When you feel fairly confident you have learnt your lines, record yourself again but leave a blank when it is your lines. It is more challenging to fill in the blanks this time when you listen back.

4. Have a line run-through as a group. Nobody is allowed to hold a script except the prompt. Everyone sits in a circle and as quickly as possible goes through a particular scene or even the entire play. Keep it brisk and emphasise that nobody needs to act while doing this. The purpose of going so fast is to sharpen reflexes and train the actors to pick up their cues quickly.

5. Stand in a circle. One volunteer goes to the centre and delivers any line. The person who has the next line says it. Continue until the teacher says stop. Then a new person enters the circle and starts from a different place in the play.

Rehearsals

General points to consider:

- Make sure the plot is clear and ALL vocabulary in the play is learnt from the outset. This is best done through simple teacher-generated exercises that students can do for homework.

- Rehearse in the largest room available, which could entail modifying the layout of a classroom or using an assembly or sports hall. The less your rehearsal space looks like a conventional classroom the better in order to minimise associations and anxieties sometimes experienced in this environment and to maximise opportunities for whole-person expression and more meaningful and realistic language practice.

- Students should be able to rehearse in the space where the actual performance is going to take place at least three times so they can acclimatise themselves to the performance space and the size of the room so they know how much they will need to project their voices. They also need to know where they will make their entrances and exits.

Tip Box

Call on the help of more able students to demonstrate an activity or take leadership responsibility in small group work. Alternatively, try giving such responsibility to more boisterous and less-motivated students.

- However long your sessions are, make sure that at least half of the time is spent rehearsing.
- If lighting, costumes, props and sound effects are required, use them as soon as possible.
- Don't start blocking (ie. determining the movements of the characters) too early. Let the actors 'feel' what is natural and logical first.
- Only rehearse the whole play in later rehearsals. Divide the play into sections and rehearse those intensively first. Allow the actors to run through the entire play without interruption at least three times.
- In general, the best approach is to let a scene run uninterrupted while the teacher takes notes. The notes are then relayed to the actors and the scene is done again.
- In order to ensure maximum visibility for the audience, a certain amount of 'cheating' sometimes needs to be done onstage:

  a. Avoid placing furniture such as tables facing the audience square on. Place it at an angle.

  b. If an actor is required to reach out with or raise his/her hand, use the upstage one ie. the hand furthest from the audience in order not to block the actor's face.

    c. If an actor kneels on one knee, use the upstage one.

    d. If two characters are having a face-to-face conversation, place them at an angle rather than square on.

    e. When an actor turns, s/he should turn out towards the audience.

    Contrary to what many believe, the above are not hard and fast rules which must not be broken but simply guidelines which should be avoided if it makes the action look contrived.

- Keep reminding the actors that the sooner they learn their lines, the more benefit they will gain from the rehearsals. Set a definite date (see example schedule below) by which you expect students to have learnt their lines.

- Ask another teacher or non-acting student to be prompt. Avoid doing this yourself as you cannot direct and prompt at the same time. To reduce anxiety, have a prompt for the performance(s) too and instruct him/her to speak loudly and clearly. The temptation is to whisper so you cannot be heard by the audience but there is nothing more frustrating for the actor if s/he cannot hear the prompt.

- Always schedule a dress rehearsal before the performance ie. a rehearsal which should be just like a performance with costume, props, make-up, sound, lighting etc.

- Eight to twelve weeks of rehearsal are probably sufficient. For the first third, you will probably only need one rehearsal a week, but as the performance gets closer, you will need to have at least two a week.

- Write up a rehearsal schedule (*see the example on p.26*) as soon as possible so the actors know when they are required, but make it clear that schedules are likely to change so make sure you have everyone's email address and mobile phone number so that they can be notified at short notice.

- It is worthwhile following the rehearsal structure suggested in this book, ie. physical warm-up, trust exercise, vocal warm-up, characterisation/ improvisation and rehearsal proper but as you approach the performance(s) and time is tight, you will find that all warm-ups will have to be brief. Never dispense with them completely though.

REHEARSAL SCHEDULE

A NIGHT OUT

Date	Room	Time	Act
May			
Tue. 6th	C-LP/11	10.30 - 12.30	Whole Cast
Wed. 14th	C-LP/11	2 - 4.30	Whole Cast
Mon. 19th	C-LP/11	10.30 - 12.30	Act I (Albert, Mother, Kedge, Seeley, Barman, Old Man)
Tue. 20th	C-LP/11	10.30 - 12.30	Act II (Albert, Mother, Kedge, Seeley, party scene)
Tue. 27th	D1-GF/02	10.30 - 12.30	Act III (Albert, Mother, Girl)
Fri. 30th	D1-GF/02	2 - 4.00	Act III (Albert, Mother, Girl)
June			
Tue. 3rd	D1-GF/02	10.30 - 12.30	Act I (Albert, Mother, Kedge, Seeley, Barman, Old Man)
Mon. 9th	D1-GF/02	10.30 - 12.30	Act II (Albert, Mother, Kedge, Seeley, party scene)
Thu. 12th	C-LP/11	2 - 4.00	Act III (Albert, Mother, Girl)
Wed. 18th	D1-GF/02	2 - 4.30	Acts I and II (Albert, Mother, Kedge, Seeley, Barman, Old Man, party scene)
Fri. 20th	C-LP/11	2 - 4.00	Acts II and III (Albert, Mother, Kedge, Seeley, party scene, Girl)
Mon. 23rd	C-LP/11	10.30 - 1.00	Acts I and II (Albert, Mother, Kedge, Seeley, Barman, Old Man, party scene)
Tue. 24th	C-LP/11	10.30 - 1.00	Whole play
Wed. 25th	C-LP/11	2 - 6.00	Whole play
Thu. 26th	C-LP/11	2 - 6.00	Whole play
Fri. 27th	C-LP/11	2- 6.00	Matinee performance
Sat. 28th	C-LP/11		Evening performance

The Performance

In the run-up to the show, make sure the play is sufficiently publicised by: student-generated posters around the school; asking colleagues to advertise it in class; and even a 'trailer' which can be performed in assembly. It is hoped that the (non-paying!) audience will be made up of fellow students, staff, family and friends.

On the evening of the performance, anxiety is likely to be high and adrenaline rushing so make sure your actors warm-up before they go on. Always finish a warm-up with a calming concentration exercise such as the one below:

Calming Concentration Exercise

Everyone stands in a circle with feet slightly apart, taking deep breaths in through the nose and out through the mouth. Stand on tip-toe for three seconds and then down again. Instruct students to focus on something in front of them, such as a mark on the wall. Repeat this until everyone can do it without wobbling for seven seconds. Then ask the learners to close their eyes and stand on tip-toe. Again, repeat the action until most, if not all, can perform the task without wobbling for seven seconds. Round this off with everyone in a circle giving each other a gentle neck and shoulder massage.

As the audience arrives, play background instrumental music and have a student-generated programme on each seat. These can be made as detailed as you like but a simple list of cast and backstage crew and a brief synopsis usually suffice.

Encourage actors to remain backstage before the performance as this can take away some of the magic of attending a theatrical performance for the audience but also the actors can lose concentration and focus if they mingle with friends before curtain up.

If possible and indeed if necessary, signify the end of the play with a blackout. The actors then go offstage to applause. The lights then come up and the actors come back onstage for their curtain call. Traditionally, the actors with minor parts take their bows first culminating with the lead(s) on their own. Everyone then joins hands and the whole cast bow together. You may feel it is inappropriate to demarcate the actors like this so, of course, there is nothing preventing the entire cast from taking their curtain call all together. The actors then go offstage, followed by a blackout and more background instrumental music.

Section Two:
Exercises

Drama-based activities for rehearsals *and* the classroom

Chapter 3

Name-learning games and physical warm-ups

For the most part, these are non-verbal activities designed to get the adrenaline flowing, generate laughter, relax the learners, develop co-operation and improve dynamics. Games force us to work closely together and as a team because they have rules which should be followed if we want them to succeed. They often require participants to touch each other which helps to lower inhibitions and they provide opportunities for students to explore the space in which they are working. Some of the games in this chapter are 'old classics' which I either learnt at school or have picked up at workshops or from students themselves over the years. You may already be familiar with some of the 'classic' exercises but I make no apology for including them, as a principal aim of this book is to provide busy teachers with a single publication that covers the whole process of staging a play so there will be no need to frantically trawl through other books and manuals for a 'good physical warm-up' or 'trust exercise'.

As teachers we continuously make choices and decisions about whether an activity is appropriate for a particular group in a particular cultural setting but do not be put off by the child-like or slightly risky nature of some of the games because, in my experience, the vast majority of learners relish the opportunity to be able to play regardless of their age and background. However, one crucial question I always ask myself when I am planning a session is: "Would I be prepared to do this if my teacher asked *me*"? and "Is this exercise culturally acceptable"? There should be trust not only between the learners but between the learners and the teacher too.

Getting your learners' attention

The activities in this section tend to be noisy and energetic so you need a fast and effective way of getting the group's attention again afterwards. This is a technique I learnt at Pilgrims in Canterbury which you can explain to your learners in the very first drama session:

You raise your hand in the air. Soon enough, a student will notice this, stop talking and raise his/her hand. Then another will notice what is going on, stop talking and raise his/her hand, and so on, until everyone is quiet with their hands in the air. Of course, the greatest thing about this is you don't have to raise your voice or indeed say anything at all.

With the more physical games, if you have a large group and are concerned about safety, have half of them act as observers while the others play and then swap over.

Note that in the descriptions of pursuit games, I refer to the chaser as 'the tagger'. His/Her task is usually to chase and touch other players. In the UK and US, this kind of game is generally referred to as 'Tag'.

One final word: ask your group if they know any games they could teach the others or even better, see if they can devise their own one together.

1. Cross the circle

Time: 10 minutes

Preparation: None

Procedure: **Stage 1**: Stand in a largish circle with your learners. Go round the circle with each person saying his/her name loudly and clearly. Then, you say your name and gesture to the student on your right to repeat your name and then say his/her name. The third person in the circle says your name, the second person's name and then his/her name. Continue this until you get to the end of the circle. The students at the end of the circle may comment that they had to remember more names than anyone else so repeat the activity but in the opposite direction. Keep this brisk.

               Stage 2: Everyone should now have a fairly good idea of each other's names. So, with you starting off as an example, make eye contact with another person in the circle and walk towards him/her. As you do this, say his/her name loudly and clearly and take their place. This person then moves out and does exactly the same with someone else. Once the group has got the idea, there should be a flowing movement of one learner crossing the circle taking another's place and so on. As this is happening, you can walk up to a different person thereby having two people crossing at the same time, then three, then four ...!

Comments: **Stage 2**: Be prepared for chaos but also a buzz of excitement! This is a very good initial name-learning game.

Variation 1: You can make it more challenging by asking learners to say their name plus *any* adjective that begins with the first letter of their name as they go round the circle e.g. A: I'm Mark and I'm manly; B: This is Mark and he's manly, I'm Dervis and I'm dishy etc. Not only is this more amusing, but it also serves as a better mnemonic. I often hear learners struggling to remember each other's names until they make the association with the adjective. They don't need to include the adjective when they do the circle-crossing stage.

Variation 2: The whole game can be played with the learners' characters' names. For the name + adjective stage, they must provide an adjective which is actually true of their character.

Variation 3: **Stage 2**: This is particularly good with younger learners: the teacher, as a man-eating crocodile snapping her arms, begins by walking towards a learner and saying her name, e.g. Gloria. Before you reach her, Gloria should say a different learner's name, e.g. Alex and approach him with snapping arms. Gloria is now the crocodile so you simply take her place in the circle as yourself. Now it is Alex's turn to approach and say the name of another learner with snapping arms, and so the game continues. The objective is not to be eaten by the crocodile!

Acknowledgement: Variation 3 is adapted from an idea by Winston and Tandy, Beginning Drama *(2001)*

Variation 4: Instead of walking across the circle, a ball can be thrown. For the first round, the throwers say their own names. For the second round, they say the names of the people they throw the ball to. As they are getting good at this, throw in a second and then a third ball.

Tip Box

Be prepared for learners to insist that *you* go round the circle naming everybody.

---

2. Alphabetical order

Time: 5 minutes

Preparation: None

Procedure: Instruct the learners to form a line at the front of the room in alphabetical order according to their first names. Make the objective of the exercise clear, ie. to learn each other's names as it is possible to complete the exercise by just asking one other person his/her name (as I have witnessed with more resourceful students). The teacher does not become involved at all in the action.

Comment: The simplest of all name-learning games but it's interesting to observe how quickly and efficiently they carry out the task.

Variation: Play the game using the learners' characters' names.

Tip Box

If they are organised, students will realise that the most efficient way to do this is for one person to act as 'director' rather than everyone milling and speaking at the same time.

---

3. Keep it up

Time: 5 minutes

Preparation: You need a largish round balloon.

Procedure: Everyone finds a space. The teacher begins by throwing or hitting the balloon in the air and saying any student's name. That student has to hit the balloon in the air and say another student's name before it touches the ground. If the balloon hits the ground, that student is out. Play the game until there are two left (who are the winners).

4. Out of your chair!

Time: 5 minutes

Preparation: You need one more than half the number of chairs as there are students, for example with a group of 20, you need 11 chairs, with a group of 30 you need 16. Form the chairs in a circle.

Procedure: Ask half the group to sit in a chair, leaving one chair empty. The rest stand **one pace back** behind a chair, including one student behind the empty chair. The student behind the empty chair calls out any seated person's name. That person has to jump up and reach the empty chair before being touched by the person behind him/her. If s/he is touched, s/he sits back down in his/her original chair. If they make it to the empty chair, their original chair is now empty. The person behind the new empty chair now calls out another seated person's name, and so on.

Acknowledgement: I learnt this game from Geoff Readman at a workshop at the Hong Kong Institute of Education in 2003.

Variation: I have since seen this game described with the people sitting down as prisoners and the people behind as guards who have to stop the prisoners from escaping. Creating a context with games such as this is a good idea because it provides your students with a more explicit rationale, and younger learners particularly respond more positively if they have to imagine they are a character.

5. Name chase

Time: 5 minutes

Preparation: none

Procedure: Each learner announces his/her name. One person is chosen to be the catcher. S/he shouts out a name and chases him/her. If caught, s/he becomes the chaser but if the one being chased manages to call out another learner's name before being caught, the catcher changes direction and chases the new person called.

Variation: This can be played using the learners' characters' names.

6. Clap-a-Name

Time: 5 minutes

Preparation: None

Procedure: Stand everyone in a circle and teach them the following
sequence, which is done to four beats:

> slap both thighs
>
> clap your hands
>
> click your right fingers
>
> click your left fingers.

When everyone can do this reasonably well, begin the game.
Everyone beats out the sequence and the teacher begins by
saying *his/her* name on the first click of the fingers and then a
student's name on the second click. That student says *his/her*
name on the first click, then another student's name on the
second click, and so on. The sequence might go something like
this:

Everyone:	slap, clap, click, click
Teacher:	slap, clap, Mark (click), Derek (click)
Derek:	slap, clap, Derek (click), Yoko

In order to give the game a clear ending, if someone makes a
mistake, they are out of the game so you end up with two
winners.

Comments: This is an excellent concentration game and also a good
illustration of how we concertina words to fit the natural rhythm
of speech. It works especially well if some of the students have
got three- or four-syllable names.

7. Emotional greetings

Time: 5 minutes

Preparation: A list of emotions expressed in your chosen play

Procedure: Elicit from your learners or prepare a list of emotions expressed in your chosen play e.g. suspicious, disgusted, surprised. Briefly discuss in plenary why particular characters are feeling in a particular way.

Stage 1: Get students milling, using as much of the space as possible. They are to greet everybody ie. shake hands and say "hello + the person's name" with a neutral tone of voice. The one rule is that they mustn't let go of the hand until they have hold of another person's hand. The general effect should be that of a kind of Waltz. Let this go on for about two minutes.

Stage 2: Follow the above procedure but this time you call out your list of emotions in turn. Each time the learners greet each other, they do so in the manner of the emotion.

Variation 1: Once your learners are familiar with the play, ask learners to greet each other in character e.g. how would Macduff greet Macbeth?

Variation 2: You can do the exercise without insisting they only let go of a person's hand once they have grasped another.

8. I went to the props cupboard

Time: 10 minutes
Preparation: None
Procedure: This is a variation of the popular children's memory game 'I
            Went to the Market' and it focuses learners' minds on personal
            possessions their particular characters own, or use in the play.
            Everyone sits in a circle. Ask each learner to think of a
            possession their character owns or a stage prop they use if the
            former doesn't apply. Go round the class inviting learners in
            turn to say, for example:

> Student A: "I went to the props cupboard and found a
> lighter".
> Student B: "I went to the props cupboard and found a lighter
> and a briefcase".
> Student C: "I went to the props cupboard and found a
> lighter, a briefcase and a baseball cap" .

            If a person makes a mistake, s/he is out of the game. Continue
            until there is one overall winner or when you have gone round
            the group at least once.

Tip Box

Insist on getting the rhythm right and the falling intonation on the last item.
Also highlight the use of weak forms and elision e.g. /ənəbriːfkeɪs/.

---

9. Stick in the mud

Time: 5-10 minutes

Preparation: None

Procedure: Choose one learner to be the tagger who runs around trying to touch as many as possible. The others try not to be touched. If a player is caught, she/he must stand still with legs apart until freed. A person can be freed when another player completely crawls through his/her legs. A player underneath a 'stuck' player cannot be touched by the tagger. Once freed, that player rejoins the game.

Comments: Some cultures may find it unacceptable to crawl through people's legs. Also, it's not a good idea to play the game if some of the girls are wearing skirts!

This is a game that encourages group co-operation as those being chased have to help each other become unstuck.

Tip Box

If the tagger isn't doing very well, nominate another tagger to help him/her out – or help the tagger yourself!

---

10. Chair race

Time: 10 minutes

Preparation: You need a chair for each student plus two extras

Procedure: Make two equal lines of learners next to each other on one side
             of the room with each person standing on a chair. At the back
             of each line should be an empty chair. On your signal to start
             the race, the empty chair is passed down the line until it reaches
             the front. Each person then moves forward one chair leaving an
             empty one at the back again. The empty one is passed forward
             and so on. The winners are the ones who reach the other side of
             the room first.

Comments: Another good example where group co-operation is required.

11. Paper chase

Time: 10 minutes

Preparation: You need a scrunched-up piece of paper or other small object

Procedure: Give one learner a scrunched-up piece of paper (in fact, it can
             be any small object such as a soft toy but the name 'Any Small
             Object Chase' isn't as catchy). Choose another learner to be the
             tagger. The aim of the game is for the tagger to catch the
             student holding the object which is continuously passed around
             from person to person as they run around the room. This should
             be a game of co-operation whereby if you see the person with
             the object being chased, you should go up to him/her and take
             the object so the tagger starts chasing you. If the person with
             the object *is* caught, he/she becomes the tagger.

12. Tag

Time: 5-10 minutes

Preparation: None

Procedure: The basic game of Tag is when you have one chaser. S/He must tag (ie. touch) another player. That player then becomes the chaser.

Variation 1: If space is limited, the game can be played in slow motion or with pigeon steps ie. one foot forward, the next step your heel touches your other foot's toes, and so on.

Variation 2: Again, if space is limited, you can insist everyone walks with stiff legs.

Variation 3: Those being chased are 'safe' ie. cannot be tagged, if they are hugging one other player, but you can only hug for three seconds at a time.

Variation 4: Those being chased are 'safe' if their feet are off the ground. Again, you can only keep your feet off the ground for three seconds at a time.

Variation 5: Play the game on all-fours or with everyone walking while holding their ankles.

Variation 6: With any of the above variations, when you are caught, you must link arms with the chaser/those already caught so you end up with a long line of people arm in arm acting as a kind of fishing net, ready to scoop up the last remaining 'victims'!

13. Grab the gold

Time: 5 minutes

Preparation: Any object symbolising a bar of gold

Procedure: Make two equal lines at either end of the room. If you have an odd number, the remaining student can be the 'caller'. Number each learner from left to right which means the two who are number 'one' are at opposite ends. Put your object halfway between the groups and stand back. Call a number e.g. "Number two"! Both 'twos' have to try and grab the gold and take it back to their line. Only once one of them grabs the gold can the other try to tag him/her. If you are tagged, the gold is put back in the centre and a new round is played. If you succeed in taking the gold back to your line without being tagged, your team gets a point. After each round, the players go to the same end ensuring they get a different opponent each time. This means after each round, the students are renumbered.

14. Group massage

Time: 5 minutes

Preparation: None

Procedure: Everyone stands in a circle and turns to their left. They give the person in front a gentle neck and shoulder massage. They say 'thank you' to the masseur and then turn to their right and massage the person who has just massaged them

Now all face inwards, still in a circle and stretch up to the ceiling – stretching the whole body. Then flop forwards with legs slightly bent. Very slowly get back into the upright position. Repeat this twice more.

Finally, with both hands, gently slap your entire body repeatedly and randomly in order to wake it up! Get students to gently slap each other all over each other's backs – this is very good for circulation!

Comments: This is best done after the group has got to know each other quite well.

This might sound a risqué exercise to some but I have never experienced a group who hasn't enjoyed it!

Tip Box

There is a tendency for the group to start walking in a circle to catch up with the person in front. Make sure when they can comfortably reach the person in front, they stop walking.

---

15. All sit down

Time: 5 minutes

Preparation: None

Procedure: Ask the group to form a tight circle with each person facing the back of the person in front of them - don't make the circle too small, though. On a count of three, everyone sits down *at the same time* on the person's lap behind. When everyone is steady, they raise their arms in the air and shout "Yee Hah", like a cowboy. And then on a count of three, everyone stands up without holding on to anything.

Comments: This only works if everyone sits down at exactly the same moment - it may require a few attempts until you get it right!

This is an ideal exercise to do straight after the Group Massage.

16. Clap and go!

Time: 5 minutes

Preparation: None

Procedure: Nominate one student (the tagger) to stand in the middle of the room with the rest of the group evenly distributed in the four corners. When the tagger claps his/her hands, the others have to run to any other corner without being touched. If they are, they also become a tagger. The winner is the last person to be tagged.

17. Knee fights

Time: 5 minutes

Preparation: None

Procedure: Students work in pairs, find a space in the room and stand
opposite their partner. The object of this game is to touch your
partner's knee(s) as many times as possible. Stand opposite
your partner with legs slightly bent touching your toes. You
have to stop your partner touching your knees by pushing
his/her hand away or putting your hand on the knee s/he has
aimed for. At the same time, you have to try and touch your
partner's knee(s) while s/he tries to prevent you. Stop after
about five minutes and check with each pair who the
winner was.

*Acknowledgement: This is slightly adapted from an idea in
Christine Poulter's* Play the Game, *Macmillan (1987).*

Variation: Instead of putting their hands on their feet, students put their
hands on their knees. If your hands are on your knees, they
cannot be touched and vice versa. You forfeit a point if you
keep your hands on your knees for more than 5 seconds. On the
teacher's signal, everyone begins trying to touch their partner's
knee(s) and guarding his/her own. The first to three is the
winner. This version is easier.

Comment: This is a great warm-up if you don't have much space.

18. Shake it out

Time: 5 minutes

Preparation: None

Procedure: Stand in a circle and shake your right hand from the wrist.
Don't shake your arm – just isolate your hand. Now shake your
left hand in the same way. Now you can shake both arms, from
the shoulder. Now shake your right leg while still shaking your
arms. Now your left leg. Now do a complete body shake
moving around in your space. Nominate a winner who makes
the most interesting sound effect to go with their actions (I find
manic chimp noises work well!)

19. Roll out the barrel

Time: 5 minutes

Preparation: None

Procedure: Form two equal teams and ask each learner to remove shoes and
             any sharp jewellery. The teams lie down in two separate lines
             on one side of the room with their heads at the same end. They
             should be close to each other but not touching. On your signal,
             the person at the back of each line rolls over everybody in the
             line until he/she reaches the front. Then the next person rolls
             over everybody until he/she reaches the front and so on. The
             winners are the team which reach the other side of the room
             first.

Comments: Only play this game if the group know each other well. Most
             groups of mine have played it with gusto but there is normally
             concern over whether people will get hurt. Tell your learners
             that if they roll over their team fairly briskly without stopping
             and that everyone relaxes, they will not hurt anyone. It really is
             great fun but naturally, if you have any doubts, choose another
             game.

20. Chase the circle

Time: 10 minutes

Preparation: None

Procedure: Form pairs with one learner as A, the other B. As make a large
             circle with a little space between them. Bs stand behind their
             partners, forming concentric circles. Everyone faces inwards.
             Choose one student A to start chasing their B (they are given
             complete freedom of the room). The object is for A to tag B
             and if this is achieved, the roles are reversed. However, if the
             person being chased stands in front of one of the other pairs in
             the circle, he/she is safe and the person at the back of *that* pair
             becomes the one being chased.

21. Chase the handkerchief

Time: 10 minutes

Preparation: A handkerchief

Procedure: The students stand in a large circle all facing inwards. Give one
             student the handkerchief to begin the game. S/He runs around
             the outside of the circle and discreetly drops the handkerchief
             behind any student. If that student realises it is behind him/her,
             s/he must pick it up and chase and catch the person who
             dropped it. The 'dropper' has to do a complete circuit and
             return to his/her original place in the circle without being
             caught. If caught, s/he is the 'dropper' again. If not, the person
             who chased him/her becomes the 'dropper'. Keep the pace of
             this game brisk as there is a tendency for energy levels to
             decrease each time there is a new 'dropper'!

             *Acknowledgement: I learnt this game from Sang Min, a student
             from Korea in 2001.*

22. Leapfrog race

Time: 10 minutes

Preparation: None

Procedure: Make two equal lines standing parallel to each other and about
             six feet apart. Students in each line stand about three feet from
             the person in front and all face forwards. Everyone, apart from
             the two at the back of each line, touches their toes with their
             heads tucked right in (to avoid injury). On the teacher's signal,
             the ones at the back leapfrog over everyone until they reach the
             front, when they touch *their* toes. The next person at the back
             also leapfrogs over everyone in his/her group until s/he reaches
             the front. This is continued until everyone has had a turn
             leapfrogging and the team to finish first is the winner.

23. Hand games

Time: 5 minutes

Preparation: None

Procedure: Put students into pairs standing opposite each other. They stand with their hands together (as if in prayer) pointing forwards towards their partner. On your signal, they randomly try to slap their opponent's hands as many times as possible. They avoid being slapped by pulling their hands back or up. After every attempt at slapping their opponent's hands, they must put their own hands back into the 'prayer' position. Finish the game when one student has slapped his/her opponent's hands ten times.

Variation 1: In pairs facing each other, student A holds his/her hands out facing upwards and student B places his/her hands face down on top of them. As many times as possible and with either hand, student A tries to slap the top of B's corresponding hand. Student B tries to avoid being slapped by pulling his/her hand in towards the body. After two minutes, swap roles. After a further two minutes, stop the game and check the scores.

Variation 2: In pairs facing each other, student A holds his/her hands out about a foot apart. Student B moves one hand in and out horizontally or up and down between A's hands as quickly as possible. Student A claps his/her hands together trying to capture B's hand. After two minutes, swap roles. After a further two minutes, stop the game and check the scores.

Comment: This and the remaining warm-ups in this chapter are ideal if you don't have much acting space.

24. Pushover

Time: 5 minutes

Preparation: None

Procedure: Put students in pairs facing each other. They should be standing about two feet apart with feet firmly together and their hands chest height with palms facing their partner. The aim is to cause your opponent to lose his/her balance by pushing his/her hands. Only short pushes are allowed. Players can push at any time – they don't have to take it in turns. Stop the game after a few minutes and check the scores.

25. One 2 twenty

Time: 5 minutes

Preparation: None

Procedure: Students sit in a circle, preferably on the floor. The object is to count to twenty *as a group* but only one person can speak at a time. You start with *1* and anyone else can continue with *2*, another person with *3* and so on. If two people speak at the same time, you have to go back to *1*. There is usually a lot of celebration when twenty is finally reached.

Variation: Instead of counting, you can go through the alphabet.

Comment: A simple but effective exercise in listening and tuning students into each other.

Tip Box

Although it's occasionally acceptable for one person to count off two numbers in one go, don't allow a student to sabotage the game by counting off all the numbers him/herself really quickly.

---

26. Chimp Snake Tiger

Time: 5 minutes

Preparation: None

Procedure: For each round, students can either be a chimp (by scratching their armpits and making loud 'ooh ooh' sounds); a snake (by hissing and extending their right arm into a forked tongue) or a tiger (by baring their teeth and sharp claws and roaring very loudly). For each round, someone in the circle counts to three and then everyone simultaneously makes one of the above animals. The object is for everyone to be synchronised and make the same animal.

Comment: To speed this game up, those in the overall minority of a given round can go out so the number of students is gradually reduced.

Tip Box

Be sensitive to neighbouring classrooms as some of these activities can be noisy.

Chapter 4

Concentration, trustwork and group dynamic-building exercises

With the kind of drama work this book is concerned with, there is the important element of performance or at least of demonstrating your work to another group. For our learners to do this to the best of their ability and for them to reap as much benefit as possible, inhibitions need to be low and there should be minimal fear of making mistakes or even making themselves look silly. Staging a play is totally collaborative. There should be the feeling that "we're all in this together and if someone makes a mistake, it doesn't matter because someone will help". Therefore, spending time on activities which build mutual trust and respect is crucial for any meaningful and creative work to take place and this, in turn, greatly enhances group dynamics and builds learners' confidence.

As well as achieving the aim of building trust between learners, the activities below offer other benefits too, such as sharpening the other senses when sight has been taken away. They can also serve to heighten spatial, proxemic and kinaesthetic awareness, essential qualities to the stage actor. Ensure that your learners are aware of these additional benefits by asking them to *feel* the space around them and the proximity of other people as they are doing the exercises. Finally, although the activities in this section require little language, they can always generate a verbal response by way of brief feedback afterwards. You may want to ask questions such as:

"Did you enjoy the sensation of walking around the room with your eyes closed?"

"How did you feel?"

"Were you scared?"

"Did you prefer being the guide or the guided?"

"Have you ever been in a situation in real life when you have completely depended on someone or someone has completely depended on you?"

A final note - safety is paramount. Some of these activities can be dangerous if they are not properly set up and supervised. If you are working with an odd number of students for an exercise that requires learners to work in pairs, use the 'odd' student to help you monitor the activity ensuring nobody is hurt. S/He can always have a turn afterwards.

1. Focus

Time: 5 minutes

Preparation: None

Procedure: Everyone stands in a circle with feet slightly apart, taking deep breaths in through the nose and out through the mouth. Stand on tip-toe for three seconds and then down again. Repeat this until everyone can do it without wobbling for seven seconds. Then ask the learners to close their eyes and stand on tip-toe. Again, repeat the action until everyone (or almost everyone!) can perform the task without wobbling for seven seconds.

Comments: This is an excellent concentration exercise and is more difficult than at first appears.

Acknowledgement: I learnt this exercise from Magnus Kirchhoff at a University of Hong Kong workshop in 2003.

Tip Box

If some find this hard, get them to focus on something in the room. When their eyes are closed, they are to see their point of focus in their mind's eye.

---

2. Chaperon

Time: 5 minutes

Preparation: None

Procedure: Work in pairs, A and B. 'A' guides 'B' around the entire space with one hand on his/her partner's shoulder and the other holding the elbow. Of course, 'B's' eyes are shut. As confidence grows, get the guides to pick up speed. They can even run.

Comments: Due to the low risk, this is a very suitable initial trust exercise.

3. Finger to finger

Time: 5 minutes

Preparation: None

Procedure: Put students into pairs (A and B) and ask them to make contact by touching forefingers. As close their eyes while Bs lead them around the room by the forefinger. After a couple of minutes, reverse roles.

Comments: Insist that the leader explores as much of the space in the room as possible. What can be interesting with any exercise of this kind is that not only do you get a feeling of the space in the room but also of the proximity of people around you.

Tip Box

With all of these 'follow my leader' type exercises, emphasise the importance of using all of the space in the room.

---

4. Follow my noise

Time: 10 minutes

Preparation: You need a list of 'sounds' that characters make from your chosen play.

Procedure: Put learners in pairs (A and B) and brainstorm as a class any human sounds made in the play you are staging (See a comprehensive list of suggestions below). All of the Bs choose a diferent sound each. The As close their eyes and are led around the room by the sound their partner is making. Touching is not allowed. If A stops making his/her noise at any point, B should immediately stop walking. When they become confident, the guide can start moving slightly further away from his B but making sure s/he is still safe. After a few minutes, reverse roles.

Variation: Students can make animal sounds (e.g. woof-woof, miaow etc) or in their pairs get them to invent a new sound e.g. a high-pitched 'beep beep' if there aren't many 'body sound effects' in your play.

Comments: Ensure the 'leader' uses as much of the space in the room as possible in order for his/her partner to gain maximum benefit from the experience.

Noises we make

yawn	sob
sigh	chuckle
scream	hum
laugh	whistle
gasp	shriek
groan	fart
hiccup	tut
snore	wheeze
sniff	hiss
cough	pant
sneeze	

5. Vampires

Time: 15 minutes

Preparation: None

Procedure: Have about a third of the group standing around the outside of the entire playing area. It's important that they are spread out. The rest are in the middle with eyes closed. The teacher chooses a vampire from those in the middle by tapping him/her on the shoulder. The vampire lets out a blood-curdling scream, letting the others in the middle know his/her whereabouts. The object is for the vampire to bite (in fact a little pinch on the neck) as many as possible. The players on the outside have to steer their friends from trouble by shouting out e.g. "Luca, turn left"! As well as helping them avoid being bitten, they also ensure they don't walk into each other or furniture. Once a player in the centre is bitten, she/he screams, dies very dramatically and then joins the others on the outside.

Comments: Make sure those on the outside know they can move freely around the outskirts of the room while shouting out their warnings/directions but they are not allowed in the central playing area. Also, make sure the monitors around the edge of the room know the names of all those in the middle because a general instruction of: "Quick, turn left"! without a name can cause confusion and pile-ups! Finish the game when all have been bitten or at a suitable time if it looks as though it will go on for more than 15 minutes.

In Augusto Boal's exercise (see acknowledgement below), when someone is bitten s/he also becomes a vampire and looks for victims (much more realistic!). Then a third, fourth, fifth vampire etc. When a vampire bites another vampire, s/he becomes re-humanised. In his (and my) experience, it is interesting to note how some people feel relief when they are bitten because they change from being 'oppressed' to becoming an 'oppressor'. For further reading of Boal's *Theatre of the Oppressed*, I strongly recommend the book below.

Acknowledgement: This is adapted from a game in Augusto Boal's Games for Actors and Non-actors, *Routledge 1992.*

6. Blind assault course

Time: 10 minutes

Preparation: You need tables and chairs

Procedure: Put the students into pairs, As and Bs. The As leave the room for five minutes while the Bs construct an assault course from the furniture in the room. The Bs then join their partners outside, bringing them in one by one. The aim is for the Bs to lead his/her A around the assault course *by the elbow and hand.* Of course, the As have their eyes closed.

Tip Box

Ensure that Bs construct a challenging and varied assault course e.g. with chairs either side of a table for stepping onto and off.

---

7. Blind circle

Time: 5-10 minutes (depending on group size)

Preparation: None

Procedure: Get the group to make a large circle. Ask one student, Sara, to stand in the middle with eyes closed. Those on the outside give Sara directions around the inside of the circle. They must not let her bump into anyone but rather ensure she moves about in all directions using as much of the space inside the circle as possible.

Variation 1: Those on the outside don't give any directions at all. They simply let Sara explore the area herself. The only time they speak is when she is about to walk into them.

Variation 2: Those on the outside slowly rotate so the person in the middle might hear, for example Peter, giving directions from one side then hear him again on the other! It's a bit disorienting for the student in the middle but fun.

Variation 3: Invite another student in the middle and then another.

8. Dialogue match

Time: 5-10 minutes

Preparation: Two-line dialogues from the play you are working on

Procedure: Pair characters up who have a verbal exchange in the play you are rehearsing. The learners choose just a two-line dialogue e.g. from *Ernie's Incredible Illucinations* by Alan Ayckbourn,

Officer: We're know you're in there English spy. Come out with your hands up.
Mum: What's he shouting about?

Make sure the learners are dotted around the room with pairs being as far away from each other as possible. Next, ask everyone to close their eyes and start saying their dialogue (it must be said in order), projecting their voices and using appropriate tone and intonation. The aim is for each person to aurally locate their partner and start moving towards him/her until pairs find each other. Once this is achieved, they open their eyes and watch the others.

Comments: This is an excellent concentration exercise as individuals have to shut out the noise being made by others and focus just on their partner's voice. If your group doesn't fall into such neat pairs, the remainder of the students can act as monitors ie. ensure people don't walk into each other or furniture. Make sure the monitors have a turn afterwards though.

> **Tip Box**
>
> - With this and other 'blind' exercises where safety is a concern, ask a student to help you monitor to ensure nobody walks into each other or the furniture – but make sure the monitor has a turn afterwards. Certainly if there is an odd number of students have a monitor rather than you pair up with him/her.
> - Students might like to fold their arms while doing certain 'blind' exercises so if they do bump into someone, the risk of hurting themselves is much less.

9. Blind car

Time: 10 minutes

Preparation: None

Procedure: Put learners into pairs, A and B. 'A' is the car (eyes closed) which will be driven around the entire space by 'B'. These are the controls: finger in the middle of the back, move forwards. The greater the pressure, the faster the car moves. Finger taken off, stop. Finger on the left shoulder, turn left. Finger on the right shoulder, turn right. Finger on the back of the neck, reverse. After five minutes, students reverse roles.

Acknowledgement: This activity comes from Augusto Boal's Games for Actors and Non-actors, *Routledge, 1992.*

> **Tip Box**
>
> Make sure it is clear that the car must stop as soon as the finger is taken off: It is tempting to take that one extra step, which might cause you to bump into someone or something!

10. Shall we dance?

Time: 5-10 minutes

Preparation: None

Procedure: Pair students off, A and B. A is the leader and places both of his/her hands on B's shoulders. B closes his/her eyes. A, who has his/her eyes open, leads B around the entire space moving forwards, backwards, sideways and diagonally. After five minutes, they reverse roles.

Comments: This would perhaps serve as a good initial trust exercise with a group because it is very safe.

11. Reform the circle

Time: 5 minutes

Preparation: None

Procedure: Everyone stands in a circle. Ask each learner to think of an animal which they can imitate (everyone should be a different animal). Each learner must remember the animal on their right and left. The students are scattered randomly around the room and stand with their eyes closed. On the teacher's signal, everyone begins making their sound. Their task is to reform the circle.

Comments: Exercises such as these illustrate to learners how much we rely on our sight but if taken away, it is possible to develop our other senses, particularly hearing. This exercise requires total concentration and a sharp ear! Tell the students to fold their arms to avoid hurting themselves if they bump into anyone. It is sensible to have two or three monitors to help you ensure nobody has an accident.

12. The trust series

Time: 10 minutes

Preparation: None

Procedure:

    a. Put students into pairs. One student is going to 'faint' (fall backwards with a straight body) into the arms of his/her partner. The faller should have his/her arms by the side and slightly away from the body. The catcher hooks his/her arms through and gently allows the partner to fall to the ground.

        Students are often hesitant to do this exercise for fear of hurting themselves and they also think they are too heavy. With correct technique, it can be done quite easily regardless of weight! The distance fallen should start off small but gradually be increased. **Safety point**: ensure the faller doesn't fall onto the knee of the catcher

    b. Put students into groups of three with A and B facing each other about four feet apart and C in the middle of them (it doesn't matter who C is facing). During this exercise, C must remain stiff and not bend at all. A begins by pushing C gently towards B, by the shoulders. C should let him/herself fall onto B's hands. B pushes C back to A, again by the shoulders. Let this continue back and forth for a minute. C should be rocking backwards and forwards from heel to toe. As the threesomes become more confident, allow the Cs to fall further and further.

    c. Have eight learners stand at one end of the room. They take off any watches or bracelets and make two equal lines facing each other. The students cross their hands and securely hold the wrist of the person opposite them. They should have created a kind of safety net. One by one, the rest of the group run up to the safety net, jump, do a half turn and land on their back into the arms of the eight. If this is too challenging, they can simply jump forwards with their arms above their heads, as if diving. When we did this exercise at school and confidence was high, we used to jump from the stage backwards into the 'net'.

Comment: These exercises are classics and have been included in many publications, but I think they will always be worth a mention because they are simple and effective.

13. Freefalling

Time: 5 minutes

Preparation: None

Procedure: Ask the learners to mill around the space in all directions. One person says: "I'm fainting!" and proceeds to fall backwards with a straight body (as in exercise 12 above). **It is essential s/he falls towards the centre of the group where there will certainly be someone there to catch him/her.** The nearest student comes to the rescue and catches the person who is 'fainting' with others also in the vicinity helping. The student who has fainted should be gently lowered to the floor by all those closest to the person who has 'fainted'.

Comment: With riskier exercises like this, safety is paramount but it's interesting to see that as the game progresses and trust develops, more and more students want to faint.

Don't work in too large a space for this exercise. If you are working in a large hall, mark out a smaller playing area.

Tip Box

- Trust exercises may be unconventional and new to some students making them reluctant to participate. Always present the exercises with self-belief and enthusiasm and eventually the more reticent ones will gain in confidence.

- Emphasise the aim of trust exercises to students ie. not to see how close to death they can take their partner(!) but to build trust and confidence in each other and develop spatial, proxemic and kinaesthetic awareness.

Many of these exercises don't require much language on the part of the student so do follow them up with plenary discussion e.g. ask: Did you enjoy that exercise? Could you trust your partner? Did you prefer being the guide or the guided?

14. Unravelling the knot

Time: 5-10 minutes

Preparation: None

Procedure: Ask all the learners to bunch up as tightly as possible in the middle of the room. They then close their eyes, reach out and grab hold of two hands belonging to two separate people. They open their eyes and find themselves in a huge knot. Their job is to untangle themselves, but they are not allowed to let go of any hands.

Comment: To achieve this (and it is not always possible!), they have to twist their bodies, walk under and step over each other's arms. Even though they are not allowed to let go of each other, they may change the angle of the clasp.

15. All freeze!

Time: 5 minutes

Preparation: None

Procedure: Students mill around the space when anyone in the group can decide to 'freeze' (stay completely motionless). As others realise someone has frozen, they too stop and freeze. The idea is to see if the whole group can freeze almost at the same time. Once everyone has frozen, everyone starts milling again until another person freezes, and so on

Comment: This is a simple but effective exercise in observation and reflexes.

16. Part of the machine

Time: 10 minutes

Preparation: None

Procedure: One student starts making a machine-like sound and simple movement in the centre of the room. Add students, one at a time, who will have their own sound and movement that interacts with the ever-growing machine on stage. Continue until all students are part of the machine! It works best if the learners imagine they are producing a factory product.

When the whole machine has been working away for about 30 seconds, go through the following sequence:

a. Tap individuals on the shoulder who should stop making their noise. Perhaps do this to a quarter of your group. It's interesting to hear the effect it has on the overall sound of the machine.

b. Ask them all to move in slow-motion with no sound

c. Move silently at normal speed

d. Give a signal to go faster, then slower and finally … to stop

Comment: This is an activity which encourages group co-operation and the team working as a whole. It also gets students to think about how the whole machine *looks* from the audience's perspective.

Tip Box

This exercise can go flat if learners don't readily volunteer to join the machine because those who are willing have to sustain their movement and noise for too long – so get students participating quickly.

---

17. Robots

Time: 5 -10 minutes

Preparation: None

Procedure: The learners form groups of three (or four if you have lots of space). In each group, one person is the controller and the other two are robots. The robots number themselves and start walking in a straight line. They only change direction on the controller's instructions. The controller gives directions like "Robot 1, turn left" or "Robot 2, stop"! If the controller is skilled, s/he can have his/her robots all moving in different directions but it is likely most will have their robots all going the same way, which is fine. Every time a robot walks into an object, s/he must start making 'beep beep' noises indicating to the controller that help is needed. The controller then gets that robot moving again in another direction.

Insist that the robots walk like robots!

Variation: Play this game in pairs but the robots must have eyes closed.

18. Blind train

Time: 10 minutes

Preparation: None

Procedure: Stand in a large circle and nominate one learner to be the train engine. S/He crosses the circle with arms moving like an old steam train and approaches one student. The dialogue goes:

Train driver: Please tell me: What's your name?

First student: Luca.

Train driver: Luca, be a carriage on my train.

Luca closes his eyes and holds the driver around the waist and is led across the circle to another student where the action is repeated. The exercise is over when the driver, who has his/her eyes open, has collected every student, who all have their eyes closed. Before you announce the end of the game though, allow the driver to do at least one circuit of the room.

Comment: As well as an enjoyable trust exercise, it is also an exercise in physical co-ordination because the movement is easier if everyone takes small steps and walks in time.

Chapter 5

Vocal warm-ups, voice development and all areas of pronunciation

The voice should be regarded as a muscle which needs to be warmed up, strengthened and developed just like any other muscle in the body. When communicating different shades of meaning, it is a vital tool so it is worth spending significant time on it.

The exercises in this section can help our learners speak with more confidence, with better articulation and resonance (quality and volume) and they can increase awareness of how the voice is used to convey different emotions (inflexion, tone/pitch and intonation). Unfortunately, largely due to the physical restrictions of a 'traditional' language classroom, experimenting with the different qualities of our voices is neglected because acting in an emotive scene or improvisation behind a desk is difficult and inhibiting. In a more open space and in the context of drama, we can start to express ourselves much more effectively with both body and voice.

Before launching into any of the activities in this section, you might like to spend no more than a minute doing a simple relaxation and loosening-up exercise concentrating on the shoulders, neck and head:

Loosening-up exercise

Stand with feet shoulder-width apart and keeping your back straight, let your head drop so you are looking at the floor. Slowly turn your head to the right then to the left. Do this two more times and return your head to the centre. Now slowly look up then down. Do this two more times. Now roll the shoulders forwards ten times making large circles. Now do the same rolling them backwards. Students get into pairs with one standing behind the other. The ones behind hold their partners by the tops of the arm, lift their shoulders as high as they will go and let them drop. The students in front should be completely relaxed and allow their shoulders to flop down. Finish off with a gentle shoulder and neck massage. Students then swap roles.

Most of the exercises here can stand alone and serve as the only vocal warm-up in an individual session but of course feel free to mix and match. You will notice that some exercises focus exclusively on the sound system of English while others explore how expressive our voices can be by varying our tone. If you have time, I recommend you do one of each in each rehearsal.

It should be noted that our aim is not to change our learners' natural voices but rather to strengthen and free up their existing voices so that they can be used effectively both in the play you are rehearsing and in real life. I have observed in classes that poor articulation leading to the listener having to strain in order to understand is often simply due to students not moving their mouths enough. This can be for a variety of reasons, for example the student may be inhibited or there is little mouth or jaw movement in the student's first language. Consequently, when doing voice work and the problem of poor articulation emerges, I tell students to exaggerate as much as possible. If a native speaker does this then of course it sounds unnatural but this is usually not the case in a second language.

1. Wake up!

Time: 5-10 minutes

Preparation: None

Procedure: Take your students through the following exercises with you demonstrating simultaneously:

Stand in a large circle and follow these steps:

a. Give yourself a thorough and vigorous face massage concentrating on your forehead, cheeks and jaw.

b. Open your face as widely as possible stretching eyes, cheeks, mouth and chin.

c. Close your face as tightly as possible scrunching up your eyes, cheeks, mouth, lips and chin.

d. Move your eyebrows up and down as much as possible. Try to move one at a time.

e. Flare your nostrils as much as possible.

f. Now wrinkle your nose as much as possible.

g. Lift your right cheek so your right eye is almost closed. Now do the same with the left cheek. Now break into a big GRIN.

h. Repeat steps b. to g. three times.

Now start walking around the space slowly (not in a circle or you'll get dizzy). When you do the following, insist the learners make sound effects too – it's more fun and helps lower inhibitions. Spend about 20 seconds on each step and encourage students to exaggerate each one.

a. Do a long yawn with your mouth open as wide as possible.

b. Yawn with your mouth closed.

c. Imagine you are chewing a big piece of chewing gum.

d. Gently pant with your tongue out.

e. Round your lips and blow exaggerated kisses at everyone.

f. With your lips relaxed, snort like a horse or make a *brrrrrrr* sound imagining you are freezing cold.

g. Blow raspberries at each other (a rude sound made by putting your tongue out and blowing).

h. Trill your tongue (when your tongue moves rapidly behind your top teeth).

i. Try and touch your nose and chin with your tongue.

j. Now explore every corner of your mouth with your tongue. Starting at the back of the mouth, touch each individual tooth with your tongue – work around the bottom first, then the top.

k. Now stop walking and - LAUGH. Laugh loudly from your belly and keep it going for as long as possible.

Comments: Don't rush each stage - let the group enjoy themselves. This sequence could be done at the beginning of all drama sessions as it is a great way of waking up the articulators (tongue, teeth and lips).

2. Connected speech

Time: 15 minutes

Preparation: A list of short quotes from the play

Procedure: Write on the board a few short quotes which clearly demonstrate examples of connected speech and discuss how stress and rhythm can affect the pronunciation of certain words when said fairly quickly, for example:

"I like fish but not chips (weak form);

"I'll see you tomorrow" (contraction);

"Did you see that film last night"? (assimilation and elision);

"You and me" (intrusive sounds: here it is /w/);

Prepare a further list of *short* quotes from the play on a handout and put learners in small groups to work out how to say the sentences as naturally as possible, bearing the above features of connected speech in mind. After five or ten minutes, invite individuals to say a sentence with you correcting when necessary.

Tip Box

You could approach this exercise from the opposite angle and provide quotes written in phonemic script with the features of connected speech inserted and learners have to decipher them and say them as naturally as possible.

---

3. Breathing and sounds

Time: 10 minutes

Preparation: None

Procedure: Before running through the following routine, indeed any of the routines in this section, it is important to adopt good posture. Ensure everyone is standing with feet shoulder-width apart and with their weight evenly distributed. Their shoulders should be very slightly back but relaxed and their bottoms pushed in. Ask students to imagine someone is very gently pulling them up by the shoulders so they should unfurl their spines. In other words, 'stand tall'. It is also important to understand that the diaphragm is a muscle that controls your breathing by pushing up under your lungs to release the air. It is important for teachers/public speakers and actors to understand the importance of its function especially with regard to avoiding unnecessary strain on the throat.

Everyone stands in a circle and follows your instructions:

a. Place your hands on your lower ribs (the diaphragm is located underneath) and breathe in deeply through your nose for a count of four, hold for a count of four then breathe out through your mouth for a count of four (try to ensure that as air is being drawn in, each learner's abdomen expands). Correct breathing like this is the first step towards developing a strong and clear voice.

b. Breathe in for a count of four, hold your breath for four and expel a **hum** for a count of four. Concentrate your hum at the back of your mouth and listen to the sound you make. Do this again and concentrate the hum on the lips (they should tickle). Can you hear the difference? Repeat.

c. Breathe in for a count of four, hold for four and expel a **hiss** for a count of four. Repeat.

d. Breathe in for a count of four, hold for four and expel a long **sigh** for a count of four. Repeat.

e. Breathe in for a count of four, hold for four, say the days of the week.

f. As in e. but say the months of the year in one breath.

g. As in e. but say the letters of the alphabet in one breath.

h. As in e. but say everyone's name.

Variation: Instead of doing steps e. to g., Hayes (1984) suggests building up a sentence to develop breath control, for example:

"I went to the cinema yesterday";

"I went to the cinema yesterday with my best friend Bill";

"I went to the cinema yesterday with my best friend Bill and we saw a really good film" etc.

Get students to provide the sentence extensions if possible.

4. Volume and control

Time: 5-10 minutes

Preparation: None

Procedure: Ask the group to think of one of their lines from the play they are rehearsing and the emotion their character is feeling at that moment, for example "In my 20 years as a general practitioner I've never heard anything quite like it" - *Ernie's Incredible Illucinations* by Alan Ayckbourn (incredulous). Then line the learners up against the end wall and explain that they should imagine they are a radio. Choose one learner to stand in the middle of the room, s/he is the volume control knob. Each student in the line keeps repeating his/her line exactly as it would be said in the play. The volume control knob moves closer and further away from the line. The closer s/he goes, the quieter the line is spoken and vice versa.

Tip Box

You be the first volume control knob as an example. Encourage the volume control knob to vary the speed of how fast s/he moves. It is more beneficial if s/he makes gradual movements backwards and forwards as this forces the others to be more in control of their voices. Tell students you are looking for subtle adjustments of volume. If the volume control knob goes right to the opposite end of the room, the learners are not to shout but project their voices in a controlled way. If the knob is very close, the group should stage whisper.

---

5. Tongue twister series

Time: 10 minutes

Preparation: A selection of tongue twisters to distribute

Procedure: The stages below are not in any particular order. This is simply a collection of exercises you can do with tongue twisters. I suggest you choose just two or three for any one session.

    a. Brainstorm as many emotions and moods as possible from the play you are rehearsing, for example excited, grumpy, romantic, terrified, bored, critical etc.

       Give each student a different tongue twister (*see p.72 for examples*). Learners mill around the room repeating their tongue twister. Every ten seconds or so, call out an emotion such as 'excited'. They must keep repeating their line with this emotion until you call out another. Then get them to say their tongue twister like a cowboy. And then like a martial arts expert in a kung fu film. For each of the emotions/ characters, encourage your students to overact and exaggerate. Let them have fun with this.

    b. Elicit or explain the meanings of some of these 'ways of speaking' and write them on the whiteboard. Choose verbs according to your students' level and also whether they might be useful in the play you are staging. Every so often while the students are milling, point to one of them and students must say their tongue twister in the manner of the

bark	declare	insist (on)	reminisce	stammer
beg	drone (on)	jeer	roar	threaten
bellow	flatter	laugh	shriek	titter
blurt (out)	gabble	lecture	sigh	urge
boast	(away)	lisp	slur	waffle
chant	gasp	moan	slurp	whine
chatter	giggle	mumble	snap	whinge
cheer	groan	murmur	snarl	whimper
choke	grovel	pant	sneer	whisper
confide	guffaw	project	snigger	yawn
coo	hiss	ramble (on)	sob	yell
croak	implore	rant	splutter	

verb.

c. Ask learners to mill around the room saying their tongue twisters with clenched teeth (this forces the tongue and lips to work harder) and then with their tongues out (apart from being hilarious, it makes the jaw work harder).

Now they (try to) say their tongue twisters with all consonants   removed

… and now with all the vowels removed!

d. Make two equal lines in the centre of the room so everyone is facing a partner. Learners keep repeating their tongue twister but gradually start walking away from their partner. They begin with a whisper but as they gradually retreat, their voices should get louder matching the distance between them. When they are at opposite ends of the room, it is important that they don't shout but rather they should project their voices with correct 'deep' breathing and a pushing out of sound.

e. Do Exercise 4 'Volume and Control', which like d. above, develops breath and volume control.

f. In pairs, Student A keeps repeating his/her tongue twister while student B tries to distract him/her using whatever means possible (but no touching)! Reverse roles.

g. As in d. but student A also has to do some kind of physical co-ordination such as rubbing their stomach and patting their head at the same time - a good exercise in concentration.

h. Another good variation to develop concentration is for students in pairs to face each other and repeat their tongue twister simultaneously, for say 30 seconds.

i. Two equal lines face each other about15 metres apart. Number the students and tell the odd numbers to swap to the other line but they are still part of their original team. Give the number ones in each team a different tongue twister each. They cross over to the other line and tell their number two the tongue twister. The number twos zig zag across passing the tongue twister to their number threes etc. The winners are those that finish first. Then get the first person in each team to share the tongue twister you gave him/her and compare that with what the last person (thinks s/he) heard!

I play this game insisting the students pass on the tongue twister with a stage whisper – of course it doesn't matter if the other team hears because they both have a different tongue twister.

Comments: You could use short lines from your chosen play but using tongue twisters is particularly useful because they allow for work on specific pronunciation difficulties your learners may have. They are especially useful for minimal pair work and consonant clusters. An excellent source is on the Web at: http://geocities.com/Athens/8136/tonguetwisters

---

Tongue Twisters

1. SIX THICK THISTLE STICKS
2. PIP AND PETE SHIPPED THE SHEEP SHIPS CHEAPLY
3. A BIG BLACK BUG BIT A BIG BLACK BEAR MADE THE BIG BLACK BEAR BLEED BLOOD
4. WALT'S VILLA IS VERGING ON THE WEIRD AND VILE
5. WEARY WANDA'S WOOLGATHERING LOST ITS VIM AND VIGOUR
6. CLIMBING CRIMES ARE LURES FOR CROWDED CLOWNS
7. JERRY'S BERRY JELLY REALLY RANKLED HIS BROILING BELLY
8. IT'S THE RIGHT LIGHT WITH THE GLIMMER IN THE MIRROR
9. THERE ARE FREE FLEAS FOR ALL THE LOYAL ROYALTY
10. SHY SHELLEY SAYS SHE SHALL SEW SHEETS
11. SHUT UP THE SHUTTERS AND SIT IN THE SHOP
12. SAM'S SHOP STOCKS SHORT SPOTTED SOCKS
13. A CRICKET CRITIC MET WITH A CRITICAL CRISIS
14. A SOFT SHOT SILK SASH SHOP SELLING SHOT SILK SASHES
15. CHERYL'S CHEAP CHIP SHOP SELLS CHEAP CHIPS
16. SHOULD SUCH A SHAPELESS SASH SUCH SHABBY STITCHES SHOW

..continued

17.   SIX SICK SLICK SLIM SYCAMORE SAPLINGS
18.   A BOX OF BISCUITS, A BATCH OF MIXED BISCUITS
19.   A SKUNK SAT ON A STUMP AND THUNK THE STUMP
      STUNK, BUT THE STUMP THUNK THE SKUNK STUNK
20.   IS THIS YOUR SISTER'S SIXTH ZITHER, SIR?
21.   THE SIXTH SICK SHEIK'S SIXTH SHEEP'S SICK
22.   I SLIT THE SHEET, THE SHEET I SLIT, AND ON THE
      SLITTED SHEET I SIT

6. I and love and you

Time: 10 minutes

Preparation: Think of emotive scenes in the play you are rehearsing

Procedure:

   a. Choose an emotive scene from your play (arguments work
      best but it could be someone persuading, complaining,
      warning, apologising, threatening, accusing etc).

   b. Put learners into pairs and discuss the details of the scene for
      a minute, for example: Who is in the scene? What's their
      relationship? Why are they arguing? What happens at the
      end?

   c. The pairs now have to improvise the short scene - but there's
      one snag - they can only use the words 'I', 'Love' and 'You'.
      Tell them they can use the words in any order they wish. A
      heated argument might go like this: A: Love, I, you, you,
      love? B: I you I love! etc.

   d. With the same partner, play the scene again but they are not
      allowed to move their heads or bodies at all

   e. As in d. but pairs lie down, head to head

   f. As in d. but standing back to back

Variation: If you are not putting on a play, have students improvise a
             heated argument between two lovers.

Comments: You could start this off by asking two volunteers to perform in front of the rest of the group, discuss their work and then pair everyone off. Make sure they play around with their voices as much as possible as they haven't got any real language to worry about or distract them. Also, allow for discussion at the end about the restrictions caused by stages d. to f. above and how it affected the communication.

7. Yes and no

Time: 10 minutes

Preparation: List about ten events/scenarios in the play you are rehearsing or invent ten (see worksheet below)

Procedure:

    a. Write this quote up on the board by George Bernard Shaw and invite comments: "There are fifty ways of saying 'yes' and five hundred of saying 'no', but only one way of writing them down".

    b. List and number your events/scenarios on a worksheet.

    c. Randomly think of each scenario and express a reaction to it using either the word Yes or No e.g. in reaction to number 2 on my example worksheet, I might say a protracted 'Nooooo', starting with a high pitch then swooping down to show sympathy.

    d. Learners number the scenarios as you say them.

    e. Elicit the moods/emotions expressed. On my worksheet, they could be: elated; sympathetic; incredulous; angry; suggestive; secretive; reluctant; depressed; bored; surprised.

    f. Learners now work in pairs trying out three or four for themselves for their partners to guess.

    g. Ask students to provide short continuations for each utterance. On my worksheet, they could be: "Yes, excellent"!, "No, what a shame", "No, come off it", "No, stop it"! etc .

Tip Box

If you feel you can't replicate a 'yes' or 'no' when asked to repeat one, you could record yourself, although this takes away from the immediacy of the exercise. In fact with intonation patterns, there is rarely only one possibility anyway so if you repeat something in a slightly different but appropriate way, it could lead to useful discussion on varying interpretations of an utterance.

YES AND NO

Listen and number the following situations according to the tone and intonation of the words 'yes' and 'no'.

Your favourite team has just scored a goal.   .....

Your friend has just told you his dog has died.   .....

You don't believe the story someone is telling you.   .....

You are telling a child not to do something dangerous.   .....

You've been asked if you had a nice weekend with your boy/girlfriend.   .....

You've been asked if you committed a crime. You want to hide the truth!.....

Your mother has asked you to tidy your room.   .....

Your favourite team has just lost the world championship.   .....

Someone is asking you boring questions.   .....

Someone has just told you an interesting piece of gossip.   .....

Now you try! Work with a partner and guess which situation s/he is in from the way 'yes' and 'no' are said.

8. Feather up!

Time: 10 minutes

Preparation: None

Procedure: Ask your students to lie on the floor with their knees raised. Tell them to let their backs *spread* across the floor, not sink into it. Take them through the following steps at a fairly slow pace. Don't rush.

a. Take a deep breath in for a count of three through the nose ensuring they can feel movement in their diaphragm (see Exercise 3), hold for three, breathe out through the mouth for three. Repeat this twice

b. Breathe in for three, hold for three and **hum** for three.

c. They are now to imagine there is a feather resting on their lips. Breathe in for three, hold for three and say: /ba:/ for three. As they breathe out, they should be trying to lift the imaginary feather just 20 centimetres from their lips (ie. the volume should not be loud).

d. Repeat this with the students lifting the feather a greater distance each time e.g. two feet, then 10 feet, then 20 feet, then ask them to try and push the feather up to the ceiling and finally ask them to push the feather through the ceiling!

e. Repeat b. and c. with /bəu/, then /bu:/ then /bei/, then /bi:/.

f. Ask them to slowly stand up and start milling around the entire space (not in a circle). Give them the sequence below. Keep repeating it until they can say it by themselves. Of course, everyone should be speaking in time with each other:

/ba:/ /bəu/ /bu:/ /bəu/ /ba:/ /bei/ /bi:/ /bei/

g. After repeating the sequence, say, five times, change the initial consonant to: /p/ then /t/ then /d/.

Of course, you can change the initial consonant to whichever you feel is appropriate to your particular group of students. *Ask them to exaggerate the vowel sounds ie. the movement in the lips, jaw and chin.*

Now working with any consonants you feel would be beneficial to your students, run through the sequence putting the vowel in initial position, eg /a:b/ /əub/ /u:b/ /əub/ /a:b/

/eib/ /i:b/ /eib/.

As above but with the consonant at the beginning and end e.g.

/ba:b/ /bəub/ /bu:b/ /bəub/ /ba:b/ /beib/ /bi:b/ /beɪb/.

To finish, go through the sequence five times using only the vowel sounds:

/a:/ /ə u/ /u:/ /ə u/ /a:/ /eɪ/ /i:/ /eɪ/.

Acknowledgement: This is adapted from and an extension of an idea in The Essential Guide to Making Theatre, *Fredman and Reade, Hodder & Stoughton, 1996*

9. La De Da Ooh La La

Time: 10 minutes

Preparation: Identify various 'functions' in your play

Procedure:

a. Put students into pairs. Write your functions on the board and ask each pair to choose one. Your list might include: persuading, complaining, warning, apologising, threatening or accusing. Pairs improvise a short scene making sure one of them is, for example, *persuading* while the other is *being persuaded*. They run their chosen scene with all blocking (ie. movement), facial expression but no dialogue. Instead, one actor mimes 'la de da' while the other mimes 'ooh la la'.

b. Pairs improvise their scene again but this time they are allowed to sound 'la de da' and 'ooh la la'. So now they must think of blocking, facial expression *and* inflexion in their voices.

c. Finally improvise the scene with real dialogue.

Comments: This is an ideal exercise in early rehearsals because you are gradually building up a scene without putting any pressure on the students to remember or articulate their lines – rather the initial focus is on producing the appropriate facial expressions, tone and pitch. It is important that all actions and facial expressions are used in order for the students to 'feel' their way into the scene.

10. Are you talking to me?

Time: 5 minutes

Preparation: None

Procedure: Write the question 'Are you talking to me?' on the whiteboard. Ask one student to read it in any way s/he wants. Then ask another to say the same sentence but in a different way (avoid specifying how it could be made different at this stage). They work in small groups and see how many *credible* ways of saying this sentence they can come up with. They should experiment with tone, pitch, volume, pace and sentence stress. After a few minutes, ask random learners for examples and discuss the context in which the question might be said in that particular way.

Comments: The idea and name of this exercise comes from Martin Scorcese's seminal film *Taxi Driver*.

11. Poetry alive!

Time: 30 - 45 minutes

Preparation: A selection of short pieces of text or poems (see example below)

Procedure:

a. Choose a suitable line from one of your poems and ask each learner to commit it to memory. Shakespeare's 'Witches' Spell' in *Macbeth* works very well with this exercise. Instruct your learners to walk around the space and *externalise* the line you have given them. In other words, they should *gesture* the words as they move around the space (see more information about *externalisation* in Exercise 19 'Make It Big Make It Small'. An example from the 'Witches' Spell' might be:

Adder's fork, and blind-worm's sting,

Lizard's leg and owlet's wing,

which lends itself well to mime and gesture.

After a few minutes when learners have experimented with the line, choose one more and follow the procedure again.

b. Give each student the following handout which is designed to encourage them to experiment with different voice qualities and effects, which they will hopefully transpose to their performance in the play later on. Students work in small groups and prepare a reading and dramatisation of their text.

Acknowledgement: This exercise is partly based on a workshop Alan Maley gave at Christ Church University College, Canterbury in 2001.

Dramatising text and poetry

Breathing   Be in control of your breathing:

    a. Breathing in the wrong place can make your speech sound unnatural and sometimes difficult to follow e.g. we do not usually breathe between a statement and its question tag or when we address someone using their name:

    "What are you doing, Peter?"

    b. Practise diaphragmatic breathing.

Volume: Vary your volume:

    a. A stage whisper can be very effective. Notice how much harder your audience listens to you.

    b. You'll stay in mid-range most of the time, but go above and below it too.

Pace: Vary your pace:

    a. Try slowing down the pace to build up suspense.

    b. Try quickening your pace to add panic or any strong emotion.

    c. Try pausing – keep your audience in suspense. Silence can have a strong impact and can be used for emphasis and it should be remembered that a pause is an integral part of the dialogue/text you are delivering.

    d. Say some of the key words sy-lla-ble by sy-lla-ble to add emphasis.

    e. Elongate vowel sounds to add emphasis.

Pitch   Vary your pitch:

    a. Pitch your voice sometimes above and below your normal key to develop *range*.

continued...

> ...continued
>
> b. Say a statement like a question and vice versa to see what effect it has.
>
> c. Make some of the words/sentences as musical as possible.
>
> Tone: Vary your tone to express mood and feeling:
>
> a. Say something critically/anxiously/timidly/aggressively etc.
>
> b. Experiment with different ways of speaking e.g. whisper, snarl or cackle

Of course, reading some of the text in unison might be effective, but also ...

- Try reading alternate lines (A, B, C, D, A, B, etc)
- Working in pairs/threes/fours, you could read two lines each (AA, BB, AA, or AA, BB, CC, etc)
- One of you could read the text while the others echo the last word/chunk/the whole line.
- Alternate the one reading the 'rhyme word' at the end of each line.
- Remember to include any suitable background sound effects (e.g. howling wind or dogs barking)

Sample text for use in Exercise 11

Macbeth

by

William Shakespeare

THE WITCHES' SPELL

ACT FOUR

Scene 1   A dark cave. In the middle, a cauldron boiling.

Thunder.   Enter the three WITCHES

Double, double, toil and trouble;

Fire burn and cauldron bubble.

Fillet of a fenny snake

In the cauldron boil and bake

Eye of newt, and toe of frog,

Wool of bat, and tongue of dog,

Adder's fork, and blind-worm's sting,

Lizard's leg and owlet's wing,

For a charm of powerful trouble,

Like a hell-broth, boil and bubble.

Double, double toil and trouble;

Fire burn, and cauldron bubble

12. Sound and action

Time: 5 minutes

Preparation: None

Procedure: For this exercise, stand everyone in a circle and begin by
             modelling an example: Go to the centre of the circle and
             produce a long /a:/ sound. You must express a specific emotion
             or idea with your voice and accompany this with a movement
             and/or gesture. There does not need to be a clear link between
             the emotion you express and the action. For example, you
             could express 'sudden realisation' with hands together in prayer
             and a curtsy! The rest of the group copies your sound and
             actions/gestures as accurately as possible. They do this three
             times. Then a second person volunteers to use the same sound
             but a completely different emotion and actions/gestures. Again,
             everyone copies three times. Then do the same with some or all
             of the following sounds: /i:/ then /ɜ:/ then /u:/ then /ɔ:/

             Finally, do the same with some or all of the following dipthongs
             ensuring students make them 'big' and long:

               /iə/ /ɔ:/ /əu/

13. Voice status

Time: 10 minutes

Preparation: You need a normal pack of playing cards

Procedure: First explain what is meant by 'status': ie that it refers not to
             social status but rather to how important or unimportant a
             person feels about him/herself. We can consider a person's
             general status, a person's different statuses in different roles e.g.
             husband, father or colleague and we can consider how a
             person's status changes during the course of a single
             conversation. For this exercise, we are going to concentrate on
             a person's *general* status.

             Give each student a playing card and tell them an Ace = a very
             low status (no self-confidence or self-esteem) and a King = a
             very high status (brimming with self-importance to the point of
             being arrogant and repellent).

a. Students DO NOT look at their own card. They hold it to their foreheads so everyone else can see it. Students mill around the space and greet each other according to the 'status card' of the people they say "hello" to e.g. I would be quite humble and submissive saying "hello" to someone whose card was a Jack, and even more so with a Queen or King and I would turn my nose up and look down on someone whose card was Ace, Two or Three. After a few minutes, students try to guess their own 'status'.

b. Give students a different card which they can look at but must not show it to anyone else. They now greet everyone according to their own status. At the end, stand in a circle and ask students to guess each other's status. If they have difficulty, ask individuals to repeat their greetings.

Comment: This exercise could belong in this chapter or the next as 'status' is a useful focus when creating a character

14. *(suspiciously)*

Time: 30 minutes
Preparation: None
Procedure:

a. Give your students a time limit of two minutes and ask them to scan your play for instances of when actors are told *how* to say a line. This is normally an adverb e.g. (suspiciously) or a short phrase e.g. (with shocked surprise). List these on the whiteboard in preparation for stage c. In two minutes, don't expect all examples to be found.

b. Stand in a circle. Count from 1 to 10 gradually raising your pitch, then count from 10 back down to 1 gradually lowering your pitch. Repeat this three times.

c. Stand in a circle and again count to 10 but this time say every third number in the manner of your first adverb or short phrase. Repeat. Follow the same procedure for all of your adverbs and/or short phrases. Don't count too quickly as the exercise can seem slightly meaningless if rushed.

Below are examples from Harold Pinter's *A Night Out*:

suspiciously	wearily	with shocked surprise	bewildered
mumbling	shuddering	doubtfully	shortly
unwillingly	irritably	quietly	pleasantly	shyly
forlornly	with an uncertain smile	muttering	
open-mouthed	wide-eyed	brightly	viciously
breathlessly	sharply	tonelessly	coughing
outraged	laughing	through his teeth	whimpering

d. Find a neutral short utterance from your play and ask learners to say it in the manner of the words/phrases above e.g. in *A Night Out*, Albert says: "What are you talking about"? Imagine the different effect this simple question would have when said wearily; viciously; whimpering; outraged etc.

15. Standing sitting lying walking running

Time: 10 minutes

Preparation: Students need to have some of their lines or another short piece of text learnt. Make sure there are about half the number of chairs as there are students positioned randomly around the space.

Procedure: This is an exercise that focuses on size and projection of voice underlining the importance of not straining the throat or tightening the neck. It also highlights that on stage, an actor has to deliver his/her lines with strength and clarity regardless of whether s/he is standing, sitting, lying down, walking or even running.

a. Stand with: feet shoulder-width apart and legs slightly flexed (not locked); eyes looking straight ahead; shoulders loose and hands free of tension by your side. Gently turn your head to the right. Then turn to the front. Then to the left. Repeat this two more times and relax.

Keeping your back straight, look down at your feet and

gently and slowly swing your head to the right, then back to the centre, then to the left, then back to the centre … and relax. There should be a continuous flow of movement. Repeat this two more times. It is important students feel the difference between the muscles being tensed and the muscles being relaxed. **As they follow the exercises below, they should aim to avoid tension in their throats, necks and shoulders**.

b. Students start slowly milling randomly around the space saying their piece of text at mid-volume. Encourage as much inflection and clarity as possible and they should also vary their tempo and phrasing.

c. With 20-second intervals, ask students to take a seat but continue saying their text. Lean forwards in their chair and change position with legs crossed etc. Still with a 20-second interval between each stage, continue to say the same or a different piece of text, and:

d. sit on the floor;

e. lie down;

f. slowly walk again *with hands behind your heads to open up the ribs*;

g. break into a slowish run.

Students should aim to maintain the original volume and clarity throughout the exercise.

16. I got rhythm

Time: 10 minutes

Preparation: None

Procedure: Write on the whiteboard the numbers 1   2   3   4

a. Stand everyone in a circle and teach them the following sequence, which is done in 4/4 time. Repeat each stage at least four times:

slap both thighs

clap your hands

click your right fingers

click your left fingers

b. slap both thighs – say: 1
clap your hands – say: 2
click your right fingers – say: 3
click your left fingers – say: 4

c. slap both thighs – say: 1 and
clap your hands – say: 2 and
click your right fingers – say: 3 and
click your left fingers – say: 4

d. slap both thighs – say: 1 and then
clap your hands – say: 2 and then
click your right fingers – say: 3 and then
click your left fingers – say: 4

e. slap both thighs – say: 1 and then a
clap your hands – say: 2 and then a
click your right fingers–say 3 and then a
click your left fingers – say: 4

f. The slap-clap-click-click sequence works very well with children's nursery rhymes such as *The Grand Old Duke of York*. It is useful when students are comfortable with the rhythm to move from the less challenging *numbers* onto *words*.

The lyrics are below and if you're unfamiliar with the tune, go to: *www.bbc.co.uk/cbeebies/tweenies/ songtime/songs/t/thegrandoldukeofyork.shtml*

Note: Do the first 'slap on thighs' on the word 'grand'

The Grand Old Duke of York

The grand old Duke of York
He had ten thousand men
He marched them up to the top of the hill
And he marched them down again
And when they were up they were up
And when they were down they were down
And when they were only half way up
They were neither up nor down

Comment: The aim is to highlight the fact that English is a stress-timed language and that each of the 'number' lines takes roughly the same amount of time to say. Students should be using weak forms elision and intrusive sounds.

Tip Box

Do the sequence five times, each time getting gradually faster. For fun, try and get students to go at breakneck speed!

---

17. Sound FX

Time: 15 minutes

Preparation: A list of 'body sound FX' (see below for examples)

Procedure:

    a. Brainstorm vocal sound effects/noises we can make with our voices. Depending on how far you are into rehearsals and how familiar students are with the play, elicit which sound effects they will need to make during their performance. You will probably have to demonstrate some and elicit/provide the actual words. Here is a sample but I suggest you don't work with so many at one time:

burp	guffaw	sniff
choke	hiccup	snore
click your tongue	hiss	sob
cough	hum	spit
creak *(e.g. an old door opening)*	pant	suck
	psst!	tut
cry	retch	wheeze
fart	shriek	whip *(ie. the sound a whip makes)*
gasp	shush	
giggle	sigh	whistle
groan	smack your lips	yawn
growl (grrrrr!)	sneeze	

b. Briefly discuss in plenary how and for what reason your chosen sounds might be made in different contexts e.g. a cough might literally be to clear your throat or it might be used to get somebody's attention.

c. In pairs for one minute only, students make different sound effects for their partner to guess. Tell them to play around with individual sounds for different contexts.

d. Select from your chosen play a piece of text or speech which lends itself to this area and get students practising it, inserting any appropriate sound FX, including hesitation devices such as 'err' and 'umm'.

e. Have a competition to see who can *laugh* and *cry* the most convincingly. Discuss why they are so difficult to do when performing and also discuss *how* you could make them more convincing (e.g. movement of shoulders, eyes and mouth).

18. Jump and kick!

Time: 10 minutes

Preparation: Have the words to *The Grand Old Duke of York* (or similar nursery rhyme in 4/4 time) available to students on a handout or on the board. You also need a relatively large acting space

Procedure:

a. Teach your learners *The Grand Old Duke of York* (or other chosen simple nursery rhyme – see Exercise 16 'I Got Rhythm')

b. Demonstrate to the group the 'jump and kick': do a small jump landing on your left foot followed by a little kick with the right foot. Then a small jump landing on your right foot followed by a little kick with your left foot.

c. Students pair up and line up in one corner of the room. In turn, each pair standing next to their partner but not touching crosses from corner to corner using the jump and kick motion and singing the nursery rhyme simultaneously and in time with each other and the jumping and kicking.

Comments: This is an exercise in synchronisation as students have to be in tune with their partner and use their peripheral vision. Equally important is physicalising the tempo of the singing through the jumps and kicks.

19. Make it big make it small!

Time: 20 - 30 minutes

Preparation: If students haven't learnt their lines yet, prepare on small slips of paper short utterances made by each character. Each utterance should be relatively easy to externalise.

Procedure: (These first two stages are optional)

   a. The whole group stands in a circle. One by one, volunteers go to the centre and do or say absolutely anything for about 10 seconds, the less impressive the better! The volunteer takes an *immodest* bow while the rest of the group whoop and clap uncontrollably, regardless of what the action was.

   b. Working in pairs, learners prepare a very short physical performance. The idea is to come up with some kind of very simple sequence of actions (e.g.. hopping from one foot to the other) but giving the impression it is very difficult – even death-defying. Each one begins with a tense drum-roll build-up and could finish with a flourish and a 'Ta dah'! Again, each performance is finished with an *immodest bow* and rapturous applause. The effect should be that of a circus act.

   c. Now give each character his/her line from the play which you have prepared and which they should be able to commit to memory in a couple of minutes.

   d. Give learners a couple of minutes thinking time and then ask them to move around the entire space externalising their line(s). 'Externalising' means acting out all or most of an utterance (obviously it is not possible with small words such as prepositions). Tell learners to exaggerate their articulation and gestures and use the full range of pitch, tone and volume: in other words, make it big!

Here is an example from *Blah Blah Blah* by Brian Marshall.

   Worker 1   **Time** (pointing to your watch) **you** (making a large arrow with both straight arms pointing forwards with hands together with an accusing facial expression) **learned** (putting on a pair of glasses, reading a book and looking studious) **to hold** (with clenched and wringing fists with a desperate facial expression) **your** (point with both hands with an accusing facial expression) **tongue** (wiggling your right arm extended as if a tongue. **Time** (pointing to your watch) **you** (making a large arrow with both straight arms pointing forwards with hands together with an accusing facial expression) **tried** (palms facing up with an imploring facial expression) **to play** (skipping around like a child) **along** (making a sweeping gesture from right to left).

Now reverse the exercise with learners minimising the gestures and articulation ie. almost to a mumble.

Comments: The rationale is that by initially externalising or physicalising text in this way, it gives learners the opportunity to literally 'feel' the words as they are being spoken, hopefully making it easier eventually to internalise. Also as a basic voice exercise, because of the accompanying gestures, it give learners time to enjoy really getting their tongues round each word in an exaggerated manner.

20. Talk at me, not to me (1)

Time: 10-15 minutes

Preparation: Each student needs to have memorised one or two short lines from the play or a tongue twister (see Exercise 5 'Tongue Twister Series')

Procedure:

   a. Learners work in pairs (A and B) and stand opposite their partner with straight arms and hands on each other's shoulders. Then, A starts pushing B across the room. B allows him/herself to be pushed but puts up a little resistance. Do not push too hard or too quickly.

   b. Learners swap roles.

   c. In turn, pairs do exactly the same but with their voices, using their memorised text or tongue twister. Insist on deep diaphragmatic breathing and forceful voice projection. It might help if they aim their voices across to the other side of the room.

d. Learners continue facing each other but now project their text to each other at the same time with appropriate tone and pitch in the voice. They need to concentrate and not be distracted by their partner and should not necessarily try and make their voice louder than their partner's as this would end in shouting, which certainly goes against the purpose of the exercise. For this stage, they are not trying to push their partner across the room.

e. Learners now scatter around the room and stand about a foot away facing the wall. Still pushing their voices out from their   diaphragm, they should imagine they are drilling a hole in the wall with their voices.

21. Talk at me, not to me (2)

Time: 3 minutes

Preparation: None

Procedure:

    a. Put learners into pairs standing opposite each other at a comfortable distance apart

    b. Announce a topic of conversation which both students speak about *at* each other at the same time. Topics might include:

        Yourself (as much detail as possible)

        Your favourite holiday

        Your best friend

        Your plans and hopes for the future

Comment: The challenge here is to maintain concentration while not trying to speak over your partner. Volume and pitch should remain fairly constant, as though they are taking part in normal conversation

22. Motorway

Time: 5 minutes

Preparation: Short pieces of text from the play and emotions written on slips of paper

Procedure:

    a. Two equal lines face each other across the room. Number the learners in order so number 1s stand opposite each other and so on. The greater the distance between them, the better.

    b. Give the odd numbers a short and simple sentence their character says in the play and the even numbers an emotion such as panic, lust or anger.

    c. They imagine the space between them is a busy motorway and they have to convey information to their partners. The odd numbers mime and/or mouth their short sentences to each other – using gesture to get meaning across is allowed. The even numbers have to sing (in order to make the noise for the motorway) a single verse of a simple song such as 'Happy Birthday' in the manner of the emotion you have given them.

    d. In plenary, check the odd numbers understood their partners' sentences and the even numbers could discern the emotion expressed in their partners' singing.

Comment: This exercise should be fun and very useful at the same time: insist that the odd numbers exaggerate the movements in their mouths and jaws when miming and that the even numbers overact or exaggerate the emotion they are trying to convey. Singing in itself is a great vocal warm-up.

23. Stretch and shape

Time: 5 minutes

Preparation: Very short utterances from the play or your own examples

Procedure:

    a. Choose suitable short utterances from the play or provide your own. If you think it will be more manageable, students can all work with the same text. See below for examples.

b. Students say their sentences as neutrally or conversationally as possible without adding any strong emotion in their voices.

c. They decide where the lowest and highest points of intonation fall in their utterances and move one pitch down for the lowest and one pitch up for the highest, so they are stretching the pitch. This usually makes it sound more musical. Do this two more times so their lowest pitch gets lower and the highest pitch gets higher.

d. Learners now say their lines with a completely flat intonation with no rises or falls

e. Repeat steps b. and c.

Examples

You shouldn't have done that.

I've got some news for you.

Do you mind?!

What are you doing here?

I was first!

Do you think she saw us?

It's just what I wanted.

I'm sorry but you can't go in there.

What time does it start?

You're making me feel nervous.

Acknowledgement: this activity is inspired by an idea in The Complete Voice and Speech Workout, *Ed. Jane Rodgers.*

24. Blimey!

Time: 5 - 10 minutes

Preparation: A short fairly unexciting text (the synopsis/blurb on the back of a script or book usually works) and a collection of expressions of enthusiastic reaction (see box below)

Procedure:

    a. Ask a more able learner to read your chosen text aloud. No doubt s/he will make a reasonable job of it so you should give appropriate praise

    b. Ask the learner to read the same text again but after each line, interject with encouraging phrases, even if they don't particularly make sense in the context. Your words/phrases might include:

Wow!	That's amazing!
You're joking	You're kidding
I don't believe it	No, never!
What?!	He doesn't/didn't!
That's unbelievable!	Get out of here!!
Blimey!	

As you do this, be very enthusiastic and exaggerated but not to the extent you completely put him/her off. To begin with, there will be lots of laughter and the benefits for the student might not be evident but when things have settled down, you should see a marked difference in the way the text is delivered because the learner should be more confident through your encouragement

    c. Write up some or all of your phrases on the board and put learners into pairs. One of them reads while the other offers enthusiastic reactions. I have found it works better if learners imagine they are telling the story to a group of enraptured children

    d. Pairs swap roles

    e. Now the first person in each pair reads his/her text again with the partner thinking appropriate reactions but not actually verbalising them. The listening student's feelings should be evident from the resulting body language and facial expression

Comment: The main aim is to encourage learners to be more confident, expressive and energetic when they read but also to illustrate how important it is to let the speaker know we are listening and are interested in what s/he is saying

To get the most out of this exercise, a large amount of overacting is required!

25. What an Insult!

Time: 5 - 10 minutes

Preparation: A collection of amusing insults (see below for examples) or
             ideally insults found in the text you are working with

Procedure:

    a. Give each learner a different insult (a search for 'famous
insults' on Google yielded hundreds of results)

    b. Individuals decide (and you can help) which words in their
utterances carry the strongest stress and where the highest
and lowest pitches fall. They can have a few minutes to
rehearse   and learn their insults by mumbling them to
themselves

    c. Learners are put in threes. Student A stands in the middle
with arms raised with students B and C holding him/her
very securely by the wrists. Student A moves in all
directions (forwards, backwards and diagonally) while being
supported by B and C. As 'A' is doing this, s/he should be
saying the insult, increasingly adding emotion to the voice,
varying pace, tone, volume and pitch. Student 'A' should
also think about creating a variety of shapes, too and could
even do this with eyes closed if it helps concentration

    d. Students B and C have a turn

Example Insults:

1. You're a mouse studying to be a rat!

2. His face is livid, gaunt. His whole body, his breath is green
with gall; his tongue drips poison.

3. That young girl is one of the least benightedly unintelligent
organic life forms it has been my profound lack of pleasure
not to be able to avoid meeting

4. You have all the characteristics of a popular politician: a
horrible voice, bad breeding, and a vulgar manner.

5. He emits an air of overwhelming vanity combined with
some unspecific nastiness, like a black widow spider in heat.

6. A modest little person, with much to be modest about.

And my favourite…which would need more than a couple of minutes to learn

    7. Curse the blasted, jelly-boned swines, the slimy, the belly-wriggling invertebrates, the miserable sodding rutters, the flaming sods, the snivelling, dribbling, ditherine, palsied, pulse-less lot that make up England today

(D H Lawrence when his book *Sons and Lovers* was rejected by publishers, Heinemann)

26. I can do that

Time: 10 minutes

Preparation: None

Procedure:

    a. Find one example in your play of sentences that contain 'can' mid-sentence; 'can't' mid-sentence and 'can' at the end of a sentence e.g. from dreamjobs by Graham Jones:

    "What can we do, nurse"?

    "I can't go through with it"

    "No Fiona, you can't help it. *(Pause)* None of us can"!

    Discuss the differences in the pronunciation and the importance of getting it right because of the possible confusion the mispronunciation of these words often causes.

    Get individuals or pairs to chorally repeat the sentences for a minute.

    b. Now each person should write one sentence about an ability they have which is obviously untrue and one sentence which the others know that person can do. In turn, learners say their sentences and the rest of the group responds in true over-the-top patomime style e.g. a French learner might say:

Student:	"I can speak 11 languages"
Group (shouting):	"Oh no you can't"!
Student (shouting):	"Oh yes I can"!
Student:	"But I can't speak French"
Group (shouting):	"Oh yes you can"
Student (shouting):	"Oh no I can't"

Chapter 6

Fluency, spontaneity and creativity: improvisation and characterisation exercises

These exercises will alert learners to the importance and benefits of thoroughly researching one's character and they will encourage them to be creative and experiment with different ways of delivering lines, altering posture and body language, walking and playing a character with different statuses. In short, they serve to illustrate how people behave and communicate with the whole person – cognitively, emotionally and viscerally.

Some of these exercises allow us to explore and develop characters whose lives we only see a small part of on stage. They provide enormous scope for improvising scenes in and outside the play and they generate discussion of characters' thoughts, words and actions which can be related to our own real-life experiences and observations of others. Indeed, many of the exercises entail doing things which will not actually be done on stage but are nevertheless essential to flesh out the character and make him/her 'real' to the audience. Students will also learn improvisation and acting techniques which are not only useful for developing character but also for real-world interaction in the target language when spontaneity and fluency are paramount.

Please note that the exercises are not in any particular order. I have left it up to you to decide which stage in your project you wish to use them. However, some of them are more advanced than others in that they require greater fluency, spontaneity and confidence and these have been marked with an asterisk (*).

1. Character profile

Time: 30 – 45 minute lesson time (interviews)

Material: Questionnaire (see examples below)

Procedure: People working in theatre and film sometimes disagree whether it's useful to invent a whole life for the character you are playing beyond what the writer tells you, but from a language teacher's perspective the process of building a character can provide a rich source of language practice material.

For example, in Harold Pinter's *A Night Out*, we only ever see the domineering Mrs Stokes at home. But does she ever leave the house when she is not on stage? If she does, where does she go? Who are her friends? What does she do? What are her beliefs and opinions? In other words, what makes her the kind of person she is? To do this, we might find it useful to create what is called her 'pre-curtain history'.

Steps a. and b. should be done in the very first rehearsal.

a. Discuss in plenary the advantages and disadvantages of creating and developing a character in detail.

b. Give each cast member the questionnaire or worksheet (below) and ask them for homework to choose ten questions (if you use the first questionnaire) they would like/are able to answer about their character. If you use the second worksheet (below), they should be able to comment on all areas. Tell them they have four weeks (or however long you feel is appropriate according to your schedule) to do this and they should be prepared to discuss and enlarge on their answers orally in a future rehearsal.

c. At a future rehearsal, put students into pairs and they take turns to interview each other. Interviewers are allowed to ask "extra" questions as they occur to them during the conversation.

Developing a Character

Name of your character:

Choose ten questions and answer them in note form:

1. What was your favourite toy as a child?
2. Describe your childhood bedroom.
3. Who was your closest childhood friend?
4. What happened to that friendship?
5. What sort of schooling did you have? Did you like it?
6. Who was your first love?
7. What kind of music are you into?
8. Describe your character's typical evening meal.
9. Where do you go to be alone?
10. What is your favourite item of clothing?
11. You always carry around a photo of someone. Who is it?
12. If you could choose one phrase or word to describe yourself, what would it be?
13. What's your idea of a good night out?
14. What's your idea of a good holiday?
15. What are your religious and spiritual beliefs?
16. What do you do before getting up /going to bed?
17. What is your education / intellectual status?
18. What is your health like?
19. What are your moral codes?
20. What is your ambition in life?
21. Who are your heroes / heroines?
22. What is your family background?
23. What major events have shaped your life?
24. What pet hates do you have?
25. What is your attitude to your work?
26. Are you happy with your physical appearance?
27. Where would you like to see yourself in ten years' time?
28. How would you like to be remembered?
29. What impact do you want your character to have on an audience?
30. Name the three key people in your life.

Comment: As well as helping students to flesh out their characters, the interview stage is also a good way to develop spontaneity and improvisation skills.

Developing a Character

Name of your character:

Carefully consider these aspects of your character's life and make notes under each heading

Social position ....

Age...

Clothing ....

Voice ....

Mannerisms ....

....

Childhood ....

....

Family History ....

....

Appearance ....

....

Adjectives to describe personality...

....

---

2. Character collage

Time: Over the course of the rehearsal period

Preparation: You will need to provide some old magazines and newspapers

Procedure:

    a. Over the course of the rehearsals, get each learner to collect magazine pictures to build a credible image of the character they are to portray. The pictures should eventually be mounted on a large piece of paper. The collage can include pictures of household objects their character might use, the style of a house, a car, clothes, jewellery, a hairstyle, pictures of people who have influenced them, leisure pursuits etc.

    b. In rehearsals leading up to the performance of the play, ask two or three learners to present their collages to the rest of the group. The presentations should only last for a maximum of three minutes.

Comments: Regularly check your students' work as you may be needed to provide any relevant vocabulary.

3. Hotseating

Time: 5 minutes per character

Preparation: None (for the teacher)

Procedure: Everyone is seated, with one learner out the front. This person must stay in character all the time as the others fire questions at him/her. They could be questions to do with the play itself or about the character's life outside the play. The learner in character must answer every question even if it's something s/he hasn't prepared for – improvise and make it up!

Comments: This is demanding and requires thorough preparation on the part of the 'character' so it's better to do this exercise later on in the project. This is an excellent exercise in developing spontaneity.

Questions might include:

    Where were you born? What's your favourite kind of music? Where were you happiest? What kind of childhood did you have? What really makes you angry? What do you really think of X (other character in the play)? What do you most like about yourself? Who or what is the greatest love of your life? Do you enjoy your job?

    It may interrupt the flow, but you could insist that a question cannot be answered unless it is grammatically correct.

Tip Box

Only hot-seat two or three characters per rehearsal.

---

4. Quick interviews

Time: 30 minutes (depending on the size of your group)
Preparation: None
Procedure: For this exercise, the students being interviewed must remain in character throughout.

    a. Individually, students write the same four questions to ask every other character in the play. By imposing such a limitation, it should encourage them to think up more interesting questions. They should be general questions and should not relate to any specific event in the play. Questions such as: "What is your favourite film"; "What kind of childhood did you have" and "What is your idea of a perfect holiday" work well. Tell learners to avoid factual questions like: "Where do you live" and "How many brothers and sisters do you have"?

    b. Divide your group into two. Half are interviewers, the other half are interviewees. Pair interviewers and interviewees up and tell the interviewers they have three minutes (be very strict with the time) to ask their questions. Interviewees must stay in character throughout. Encourage the characters to elaborate on their answers as much as possible and to remain in character all the time. After three minutes, call 'time up' and ask interviewers to find another interviewee. They ask their new partner the same questions. This is repeated until everyone has been interviewed. If you have an odd number, two interviewers can interview one person.

    c. The whole exercise is repeated with interviewers becoming interviewees and vice versa.

    d. Round the exercise up with an informal vote as to who: the kindest/selfish/most interesting/boring person was. You could also vote on which character they would most/least like to date/have as a friend/a teacher/a parent etc.

5. Soliloquy*

Time: 2 minutes per student in class
Preparation: None (for teacher)
Procedure:

    a. Explain to your learners what a soliloquy is. According to the *Longman Dictionary of English Language and Culture*, it is: (an act of) talking to oneself alone, esp. a speech in a play in which a character's private thoughts are spoken to those watching the play. Tell students that as they begin to create and continue to develop their character, they should prepare a two-minute soliloquy, which they will 'present' to the group at a future rehearsal. Their soliloquies should not only be biographical but should also refer to actions, events and characters within the play itself. As a guideline, learners can use some of the questions and ideas in Exercise 1, Character Profile, as well as comments on how they feel about other characters in the play.

    b. At future rehearsals, preferably near to the performance, ask two or three individuals to deliver their soliloquies. Emphasise that they should be delivered in character.

6. Out the bag

Time: 20 minutes
Preparation: You will need scrap paper and pens
Procedure:

    a. Put learners into groups of three or four and ask them to choose just one of the characters from the play you are rehearsing. Different groups can choose different characters.

    b. Ask them to think of a bag this character might typically use, e.g. a doctor would probably take a briefcase to work. Then as quickly as possible, ask each group to jot down on a piece of paper a list of contents their chosen bag might contain e.g. in a doctor's bag: mobile phone, stethoscope, pen, diary.

    c. Take the list of objects from them and allot one object per student and tell them they are to imagine they actually are this object and they are all together in their respective bags.

d. Get the exercise going by telling them to simply chat about anything they wish: the owner of the bag and the way they are treated by him/her, the weather - anything!

e. Go around each group and call out an object from each bag e.g. mobile phone. The mobile phone leaves the group imagining it has been removed by the owner during which time the others in the bag continue chatting, perhaps speculating why the phone has been taken out. After about a minute, send the phone back in and s/he has to recount to the others what has just happened e.g. "You'll never guess what. He's just had a terrible argument with his wife" etc.
Continue the exercise until all objects have had a turn being taken out.

Comments: Due to the light-hearted nature of this exercise, it's better done in the early stages of your drama project, especially as students will probably be working on a character other than their own. Also, learners might get too bogged down and stymied with details of what has been established for particular characters in the play later on in the project. Let them enjoy the exercise and make up all sorts of things about the characters, even if they are totally inaccurate. Their ideas can be accepted or rejected at a later stage. Another reason for doing it early on is that it allows for generalisations to be formed, which can be discussed and narrowed down later.

Keep the pace of the exercise brisk and don't force students to improvise for too long.

Acknowledgement: This is based on an idea in Theodora's *Idea That Work in Drama* (1990)

7. Character visualisation

Time: 10 minutes

Preparation: Scatter some tables and chairs around the room

Procedure: Ask each learner to think of one or two of his/her lines from the play.

a. Students mill around the room independently in character projecting their lines using appropriate expression in their voices.

b. After a minute, instruct them to stop walking and to carry out everyday activities in an imaginary mirror, always remaining in character. You may want to take them through the visualisation like this:

"Look at yourself in the mirror. Look carefully. Look at your hair, your face, the way you are standing, the way you are holding your head. Now run the tap and wash your face thoroughly. Now have a shave or put on some make-up. Now brush your teeth. Now brush your hair. Keep looking at yourself all the time and visualise your character. Look at your body. What does it look like? Now move around the room. Practise sitting down and standing up. Go and look out the window. Sit on the floor. Get on your hands and knees and try to find something you've lost. Sit at a table and pick up a book. Start reading it. What kind of book is it? Now get up and carry your chair to the other side of the room. Sit down and relax ..."

Finally, put students into small groups to briefly discuss what they found out about their character.

Comments: What may be useful is in one session go through the above sequence instructing the learners to be themselves and then in the next session go through it in character. Do not rush this exercise because it's essential learners think about how or in what manner these simple activities are carried out. Also, there is often the tendency on stage to rush these kinds of everyday actions. Ask learners how long it takes them to brush their hair etc in real life. If such actions feature in your play then they should also be done in real time and convincingly.

8. Freeze emotion freeze object

Time: 10 minutes

Preparation: A list of emotions from the play and events/objects

Procedure:

a. Elicit from the group or have a pre-prepared list of emotions and moods from the play. Your list might look something like this:

bored	aggressive	gloomy	touchy	flustered
	belittled	aloof	confused	
embarrassed	remorseful		smug	upset

Ask the learners to start milling around the room (not in a circle but in all directions), using as much of the space as possible. After about every ten seconds, call out one of the emotions. The learners should immediately freeze expressing the given emotion with their bodies and faces. Encourage them to be as expressive as possible. Hold the position for five seconds and start milling again, and so on until you have got through your list.

b. Put learners into pairs. Give all pairs the same object or event from the play e.g. computer, bus, love, murder, holiday. They have three minutes to prepare a photographic image of that object/event. When they are ready, ask them to show their images to the other groups in turn.

c. Put them in threes with a different object or event, and then fours. Each time, get each group to show their images to the other groups and compare the different groups' interpretations

d. This step can be carried out at any time during a. – c. When a group has frozen, tap one student at a time on the shoulder to offer a short piece of appropriate dialogue – regardless of whether they are people or objects in the scene!

Comment: Apart from being a useful activity for exploring how to communicate emotions with our bodies and faces, it could also help the teacher who lacks props e.g. if you need a computer in the play and haven't got one, get the actors to make one out of their bodies.

Tip Box

As with many of the exercises in this section, a lot of the language benefits here come from discussion and negotiation. The groups should produce a single unambiguous image. I once gave a group the word 'love' and they created an image of a couple in church getting married by a priest. If a stranger had walked into the room, s/he would have wrongly guessed that the word I had given them was 'marriage'.

9. Yes, Let's!

Time: 10 minutes

Preparation: None

Procedure: Brainstorm clearly-definable actions from the play you are
             rehearsing e.g. digging a hole, changing a lightbulb, reading a
             book, looking for your keys etc. Write these up on the
             whiteboard.

             Ask students to mill around the room. Every so often, someone
             calls out, for example, "Let's change a lightbulb". Everyone
             stops walking and shouts "Yes, let's!" and mimes changing a
             lightbulb or whatever action has been called out. The game is
             over when all of the actions have been called out.

Comments: Don't allow for half-hearted attempts at the mimes. Insist your
             learners make them as convincing and realistic as possible

10. Outside the Play*

Time: 10 minutes

Preparation: None

Procedure: Group characters according to whether they are in any way
             connected in the play you are rehearsing, e.g. part of the same
             family or work colleagues. They don't necessarily have to
             speak to each other in the play. I have done this exercise when
             rehearsing for *Dreamjobs* by Graham Jones in which a group of
             school friends (all female) are all waiting to see the
             Employment Officer.

             Ask each group to imagine they are in a scene which is not in
             the play e.g. for *Dreamjobs*, in the school canteen. They now
             have to improvise a short scene in this new environment
             remaining in character throughout. You could either give them
             something specific to talk about e.g. in *Dreamjobs* I asked the
             girls to imagine they had all had their interviews with the
             Employment Officer and were in the school canteen discussing
             the outcome or you could just set the scene up, let it run and see
             what happens!

Comments: If your group doesn't divide up neatly ie. if you have one or two students who don't really fit into any group, you can use them by asking them to enter the scene and do something unexpected, like spilling a drink or introducing him/herself as an old friend. Once the scene is running, try whispering into people's ears asking them to do something unexpected to see how the others react e.g.. "burst out crying" or "run out of the room, then run back in again". This kind of improvisation sharpens reactions and develops spontaneity and creativity.

11. Taglines and trailers*

Time: At least 1 hour of class time or gradually over the period of rehearsals

Preparation: Tagline quiz sheet (see below) and example movie trailers (optional). Students need to know the play you are doing well to do this exercise.

Procedure:

a. Ask whether anyone knows what a movie tagline is (these are the short phrases found at the bottom of movie posters designed to entice people into seeing the film and they, to an extent, summarise the film). Elicit from the class any taglines they might be able to recall.

b. Give the class a movie tagline quiz (see example below) and ask them to complete it in groups. You can find any tagline you want at www.imdb.co.uk. Alternatively, submit 'movie taglines' into your internet search engine and you will find many websites to choose from. Make this stage brisk and go over the answers in plenary.

c. Tell the groups they are to imagine they are making a film of the play you are staging and they have been given the job of providing a catchy tagline for it. After 10 to 15 minutes, ask individual groups to share their ideas and vote on the best one.

d. Their next task is to prepare a trailer and a voiceover, which they will perform. The trailer should last for a minute and should summarise the 'movie', introduce the main characters in a captivating way, focus on the main events and not give too much of the plot away. Tell them to think carefully about the final frame of the trailer. Give them a twenty-minute time limit. Then invite individuals to perform their voiceovers in a suitable voice. If you have internet access, go to www.imdb.co.uk and find the 2002 movie *Comedian*. Go to the film's trailer and you will see movie trailers being sent up, complete with gravely voice and full of clichés.

Movie Tagline Quiz

Match the Tagline with the Movie

1. 'An adventure 65 million years in the making' (clue: Steven Spielberg)	
2. 'She walked off the street, into his life and stole his heart' (clue: Julia Roberts)	a. Speed
	b. Titanic
3. 'Get ready for rush hour' (clue: Sandra Bullock)	c. Gangs of New York
4. 'For Harry and Lloyd everyday is a no-brainer' (clue: Jim Carrey)	d. Jurassic Park
5. 'Collide with destiny' (clue: Leonardo de Caprio)	e. The Matrix Reloaded
6. 'America was born in the streets' (clue: Daniel Day Lewis)	f. Terminator
7. 'The Machines will rise' (clue: Arnold Schwarzenegger)	g. Rocky
8. 'Free Your Mind' (clue: Keanu Reeves)	h. Hulk
9. 'The inner beast will be released' (clue: Ang Lee)	i. Pretty Woman
10. 'His whole life was a million-to-one shot' (clue: Sylvester Stallone)	j. Dumb and Dumber

Key: 1d, 2i, 3a, 4j, 5b, 6c, 7f, 8e, 9h, 10g

Comment: You may feel that rehearsal time is too precious to devote so much time to an exercise. An alternative is for students to work in their groups outside class time and present their work to each other as you are nearing the performance. You could even choose to perform some of the pieces in school assembly in the run up to performance – voiceovers and/or acting

---

Tip Box

Many of the exercises in this section can be modified to give learners guidance and support when doing role-plays and simulations in general English classes to help them flesh out characters and make them more realistic.

---

12. 90-second play*

Time: 20 – 30 minutes

Preparation: None

Procedure: Students need to be very familiar with the play in order to do this exercise.

   a. Put students into small groups and ask them to write a plot skeleton of your chosen play. In other words, they need to identify the key moments in the story. They should write in note form. It is important they don't just choose certain whole scenes from the play. Their skeleton should consist of scenes or moments within the *actual* scenes.

   b. Give each group about 20 minutes to prepare a 90-second dramatisation of your play. They need to decide how they are going to dramatise the key moments from the first stage and who is going to play which part. Students may need to double up ie. play more than one character, which makes the exercise much more fun (learners don't have to play their own characters).

   c. Each group performs their version.

   d. Discuss in plenary each group's version focussing mainly on the key moments each group chose. Guide the discussion asking questions such as why they chose certain moments/scenes and not others. Why did they include certain characters and not others? What for you is the key moment in the play?

Comments: The principal aim of this exercise is to enable learners to produce a slick energetic ensemble piece of drama. They should be able to complete the play within the 90 seconds so be VERY STRICT with timing. It makes the exercise more frantic and fun.

Variation: I have done this exercise in general drama classes getting learners to abridge a well-known fairytale such as *Little Red Riding Hood* or *Jack and the Beanstalk*.

After they have performed their 90-second version of the tale, individuals who played the main characters can improvise giving witness statements to another student who acts as a police officer.

For example, Little Red Riding Hood can explain to the police officer, in character, what happened to her and her grandmother, and the Wolf can interject and interrupt, in character, and give his/her side of the story.

Tip Box

Encourage students to create props and furniture using their bodies and also to provide off-stage sound effects if appropriate.

Acknowledgement: The idea for this came after watching The Reduced Shakespeare Company's show The Complete Works of William Shakespeare, *condensing all 37 plays into 97 minutes.*

13. Making it real

Time: 20 minutes

Preparation: None

Procedure: Put two rows of chairs at the front of the room resembling a doctor's waiting room. Ask five or six students to come to the front of the class to be patients waiting to see the doctor. Tell them that they do not know each other. Then stand back and let them improvise for one or two minutes. What often follows is a show of self-conscious unnatural behaviour which forces some into feeling they have to be entertaining or interesting: they might start complaining in a very animated fashion about the weather or having to wait so long to the person next to them; some might talk about how angry their boss is going to be if they are late back to work. Next, ask the observers for any comments and they usually reply that it was amusing and entertaining. "But was it realistic"? I ask. I then ask them to think back to a time when they actually were in a doctor's waiting room and to recall their actual behaviour and emotions. Five or six more improvisers come to the front and repeat the exercise. This time, we have a line of people sitting, shuffling, stealing a glance at the person next to them or at their newspaper, looking at their watch but for the most part, not saying a word. This might not be as overtly entertaining as the first version but it portrays what happens in real life and in fact to my mind is far more interesting to watch. The 'audience' should be observing and empathising with the actors: "Yes, isn't it boring waiting for the doctor".

Comment: This is an exercise I did when producing Ernie's *Incredible Illucinations* by Alan Ayckbourn because the first scene is in a doctor's waiting room! In your chosen play, try and find a similar scene which could so easily be 'hammed' e.g. waiting for a bus or at a party.

14. Stanislavski's 'system'*

Time: 90 minutes (less if you don't cover all the elements below)

Preparation: Familiarise yourself with the background information below and if possible with some of Stanislavski's own publications. This group of exercises focuses on some key elements of Stanislavski's teaching. Before embarking on any, make sure you are familiar with them and confident about presenting them to your learners. Of course it is up to you how much background information you think your learners need but I advise you to supplement your presentation with plenty of examples. It should be relatively brief and could even be done in the mother tongue.

Constantin Stanislavski - Background information

There have been several influential contributors to actor training in the West (and to an extent the East) over the past century but none is more often quoted and significant than the Russian actor and director Constantin Stanislavski (1863–1938) who spent his life in search of ways actors could supply truthful feelings under given circumstances to the characters they were portraying. He analysed what constituted good acting and published his findings in three seminal works: *An Actor Prepares*, *Building a Character* and *Creating a Role*. The three books set out how to help actors fully develop a character which can convince an audience of its semblance to reality and provoke a human response. It is his 'system' which is endorsed by many acting schools and colleges throughout the West and which was exported to the US and adapted for screen actors at the Actor's Studio in New York, which trained notables such as Al Pacino and Robert de Niro. The American version is what we refer to today as 'Method Acting'.

Super objective, motivation and necessity

It was Stanislavski's suggestion that actors try to identify their character's super objective in a play. For example, Macbeth wants to be king and will do anything to achieve this and almost everything that character does in the play feeds his Super Objective. In Harold Pinter's *A Night Out*, Albert's Super Objective is to escape the clutches of his domineering mother. Stanislavski suggests we consider how a character's behaviour feeds his/her Super Objective, how it relates to the play as a whole and how it can bring an extra dimension and perspective to an actor's performance. At a narrower level, we can consider a character's Motivation, that is what drives him/her to say certain things and behave in a certain way, usually at specific points in the play. Finally, Necessity refers to things a character needs in life to survive, such as respect, money or friendship. It is worth devoting a lot of time to discussing, exploring and experimenting with characters' motivations and necessities as factors such as these affect behaviour, interaction and communication.

Activities: Choose a short section of your play and act out the same short scene three or four times but each with a different motivation behind the words. The thought process going on behind the dialogue can have an important impact on the way the words are delivered, how the character behaves and the impact it has on the listener. In groups, discuss the thought process going on behind the characters' words in your chosen section. In drama terminology, this is called 'thought tracking'. Below is an example from *A Night Out* with example motivations.

Mrs Stokes	You're going out?
	("I know you're going out really but I *want* you to stay in with me tonight")
Albert	You know I'm going out.
	("I'm getting angry but won't show it – I want Mum to accept this but not get upset")
Mrs Stokes	But what about your dinner?
	("I *want* to emotionally blackmail him! I'll do anything to keep him at home)

This exercise can only be done when the group is very familiar with their characters and the play. Ask students to spend 10 to 15 minutes listing their own character's Necessities. Remember, these refer to what your character needs in life to get by. Students' lists should not only include material objects such as money or a large house but they should also consider needs such as: love; occasional solitude; competition; fresh challenges etc. When the time is up, discuss their lists in plenary, which should be justified. Note that this kind of work should be on-going throughout the rehearsal period.

The 'Magic If'

Stanislavski talked of the 'Magic If', requiring his actors to imagine what *they* would do in their character's given situation. This not only encouraged them to play and experiment with characters and scenes but also helped bring truth to the performance. However, a common misconception of his 'system' is that he urged the actors to be their character. Rather, he asked them to live their part with the 'Magic If''.

Activity: This is an activity or technique you can use during rehearsal. If you see a learner is not really playing a particular scene convincingly, ask him/her questions such as:

"What would *you* do/say if *you* were in this situation?"

"How would *you* react if someone said this to *you?*"

"How would *you* feel if someone said/did this to *you?*"

This is related to the previous section on Motivation in that the way we feel impacts on the way we deliver speech and interact with others.

Emotion memory

Activity: An actor's greatest resource is his/her own experience of the world. Stanislavski spoke about 'Emotion Memory' which required his actors to recall their own life experiences which were either the same or similar to what was happening to their character and bring these *emotion memories* to their acting. Take your time as you guide students through the following 'sense' exercise and ask them to discuss in small groups which senses were easiest to recall:

Ask your learners to sit as comfortably as possible with hands on their laps or by their sides and their eyes closed. Slowly take them through some/all of the exercise below giving them approximately 15 seconds for each:

Picture: a house where you once lived/an elephant/a famous building in your country/a sky full of stars.

Hear: a dog barking/footsteps climbing stairs/feet crunching in snow.

Smell: an orange/the sea/rain on wet grass/petrol.

Taste: chocolate/your favourite dish/grapefruit juice.

Touch: stroke a cat/a very hot drink on your tongue/the surface of a pineapple.

Recall EVERYTHING: imagine a familiar journey to a shop/school then describe it in as much detail as possible to your partner.

Recall emotions: an enjoyable party/a time when you were angry/felt ashamed/terrified/received an unwanted gift.

15. Status

Time: 60 minutes

Preparation: Familiarise yourself with the background information below

                      A pack of playing cards (optional)

Background Information:

Keith Johnstone is principally a theatre director and internationally-renowned improvisation coach and has produced two vitally important publications on the art of improvisation, *Impro* and *Impro for Storytellers*. He is probably most notable for his work on the role of *status* in oral communication.

Here, *status* refers not to social status but rather to how important or unimportant a person feels about him/herself. We can consider a person's general status, a person's different statuses in different roles e.g. husband, teacher or colleague and we can even consider how a person's status changes during the course of a single conversation. Johnstone notes that conversation flows much more naturally and for longer if each speaker continually raises and lowers his/her status during the course of a conversation thereby relating your behaviour to your co-improviser's. He calls it the see-saw effect. This is a useful device to point out to learners in order to maximise speaking practice when improvising or role-playing.

A lot of comedy derives from characters with a low social status but a high personal status. Think of a scene with an office cleaner who has a high personal status talking to a Chief Executive who is as meek as a lamb ie. has a low personal status. Imagine the cleaner telling her boss off for the mess in the office and the executive mumbling humble apologies!

When improvising, it is helpful to provide a scale: 1 = a very low status (no self-confidence or self-esteem) and 10 = a very high status (brimming with self-importance to the point of being arrogant and repellent). I use this scale if I want to control which status I want improvisers to adopt but an alternative random approach is for the student to pick a playing card: Ace is low, King is high.

Activities:

a. Briefly run through what *status* means for our purposes and supplement your explanation with examples or try to elicit ideas from the group e.g. people with a high status often speak more slowly and keep their head and eyes still when speaking. People with a low status often speak faster and keep moving their head and eyes and allow hesitation in their voice.

b. The first exercise is designed to be straightforward and not linguistically challenging. Ask for a volunteer or nominate a student and thank him/her for volunteering! Place a chair at the front of the room in full view. Tell the student s/he has a status of 1 and should enter the room, go up to the chair, sit down and say "Good afternoon/morning. My name is ……… ." The whole action should be carried out in the status of 1. Students who have never done this kind of work before (and most if not all haven't in my experience) usually underplay it. If you see this with your first "volunteer", certainly don't stop the action. Let it run and follow it up with discussion. Statuses of 1 and 10 are absolute extremes and fortunately in life are extremely rare. This is an example of how a person, say Dervis, with a status of 1 might carry out the exercise: Dervis begins with a timid knock on the door. Then another. He then reluctantly opens the door and peers into the room. He looks at the people with fear in his eyes. He looks at the chair with just as much fear as he starts to very slowly creep up to it. He eventually perches himself on the edge and without making any eye contact whispers his name before scampering out of the room. If he had a status of 10, he wouldn't even bother knocking. He would stride up to the chair, stand on it and declare his greeting!

I suggest you repeat this exercise three or four times with different learners playing different statuses. Then, put students into groups of four or five depending on how big your group is and ask them to practise going from 1 to 10 on different chairs placed around the room.

c. Ask for two volunteers or invite two students to come to the front and introduce the scene: Student A is interviewing Student B for a teaching post. Secretly whisper a status into each actor's ear (from 1 to 10) and their task during the improvisation is to achieve their given number. Working with the higher and lower numbers is initially advisable in order to clarify the purpose of the exercise. Let the scene run for about a minute and ask the group to guess which status you assigned each character. I usually start by giving the interviewer a status of 10 and the interviewee a status of 1. Repeat this two or three more times with different students and statuses and don't be afraid to play around by giving the interviewer a very low status and the interviewee a high one or both participants a very high one. After each short improvisation (about two minutes) discuss the effect status had on the interaction and how successful the communication was.

Of course the point is to play your own character in the play with different statuses until you arrive at what you personally feel is the right one.

Acknowledgement: This is partly based on ideas in The Essential Guide to Making Theatre, *Fredman and Reade (1996)*

16. Blocking and accepting*

Time: 60 minutes

Preparation: None

The ideas presented here are also based on the work of Keith Johnstone: in improvisation a block is when you prevent the action or narrative from developing or moving forwards by, for example, disagreeing with your co-improviser, rejecting his/her ideas or simply ignoring what s/he has said and following your own agenda. *Accepting* is when we simply say 'Yes' to an 'offer' i.e. anything s/he says, and go in the direction our partner seems to want to go. Johnstone noted with inexperienced native-speaker improvisers and trainee actors that they would quickly reach a stalemate point in the improvisation because they were trying to be clever, original and funny. Johnstone was famous for shouting: "Be boring"! at his improvisers when he felt they were trying so hard to be entertaining that communication collapsed and became meaningless. I have noticed with EFL students that they tend to block offers probably because they lack confidence in themselves and are not in control of where the scene is leading. Blocking gives an improviser control over the improvisation. For example, I have witnessed one improviser commenting on the terrible weather and the other blocking it by saying that it was a beautiful sunny day! This of course is absurd and immediately stymies your co-improviser. To maximise speaking practice, emphasise how important it is to accept most offers. Only then can the narrative move forward.

Activity: The scene is a clothes shop. One student is the shop assistant and the other is the customer. Tell them that they are to *accept* everything the other says (or as Johnstone calls it 'offers'). In other words, whatever your co-actor throws at you, you have to go with. Introduce one rule though, which is despite this, the customer does not want to buy any of the clothes offered (because the improvisation would be over after a few seconds)! I usually let this scene last for a couple of minutes. Then invite two more students to repeat the scene but this time, the shop assistant *accepts* everything and the customer *blocks* everything. I repeat this once more with both characters blocking everything the other says. In plenary, discuss the three scenes and comment on what resulted: you will probably conclude that although the last version was interesting and entertaining to observe because there was a lot of conflict, the first version lasted the longest because they were both accepting. This brought creativity to the scene and allowed the narrative to move forwards. It should become clear that alternately 'offering' and 'accepting' leads to heightened creativity and co-operation between the participants. Generally in improvisation, there should be a certain amount of blocking but for our purposes as language teachers, this should be outweighed by mostly accepting.

You may find it useful to supply your learners with the general guidelines below:

Guidelines for Improvisation:

- Maintain concentration throughout.
- Don't laugh (*corpse* in acting terminology). It immediately breaks concentration.
- Listen to what is being said to you and *react* accordingly (don't have your own agenda).
- You don't have to project your voice all the time, but make sure your audience can comfortably hear you.
- Observe and be sensitive to what is happening around you.
- Don't worry about looking silly.
- Don't mask/upstage other performers.
- Make good use of the space.
- Adopt a clear status.
  High status = slow, Low status = fast
  High status = keep head and eyes still and talk in complete sentences
  Low status = keep moving head and eyes and allow hesitation in voice
  Pitch your status a little below or above your co-improviser's
- Aim to be spontaneous rather than original.
- Accept what other performers are doing and saying and build on it (don't block too much).

17. All change!

Time: 15 minutes

Preparation: Everyone's costumes should be packed into either of two suitcases

Procedure:

a. Pack half of the cast's costumes into one suitcase and the other half of the cast's into another.

b. Divide the cast up into teams A and B. Each team stands in line at one end of the room with their corresponding suitcase at the other. Make sure all of team A's costumes are in their corresponding suitcase and the same for Group B. Only include costume items that can be put over the top of students' own clothes.

c. Tell the group that they have all overslept and are late for a very important job interview. Their alarm has just gone off and they have to get dressed as quickly as possible. The first player in each line runs to their suitcase, finds their costume, puts it on and runs to the back of their line. When the first player has arrived at the back of the line, the second player runs to the suitcase, finds their costume, puts it on and runs to the back and so on. This continues until everyone has changed into their costume. The team to finish first are the winners.

Comments: It is possible very few characters have costume items that can be put over the top of students' own clothes in which case, it is not worth trying to play this game.

This could be used as a physical warm-up but I've included it in the acting section because characters occasionally have to make quick costume changes and it is a good idea to provide the cast with practice.

18. It's all in the face!

Time: 30-45 minutes

Preparation: None

Procedure:

a. Take your students through the following exercises with you demonstrating at the same time. Don't rush each stage. Stand in a large circle and follow these steps:

- Give yourself a thorough and vigorous face massage concentrating on your forehead, cheeks and jaw.

- Open your face as widely as possible stretching eyes, cheeks, mouth and chin.

- Close your face as tightly as possible scrunching up your eyes, cheeks, mouth, lips and chin.

- Move your eyebrows up and down as much as possible. Try to move one at a time.

- Flare your nostrils as much as possible.

- Now wrinkle your nose as much as possible.

- Lift your right cheek so your right eye is almost closed. Now do the same with the left cheek.

- Now break into a big GRIN with wide eyes. Demonstrate this and discuss possible reasons why someone might have this facial expression e.g. receiving a much-wanted gift.

Facial expressions:

b. Write up some or all of these words on the whiteboard according to the level of your class and the usefulness of the words.

frown   gawp   gaze   glare   grimace   leer   pout

scowl   smirk   sneer   wince

Demonstrate your chosen words with students copying. Insist that they 'get it right'. Discuss why people might make these facial expressions. Can any of them be used in the play you are producing? Brainstorm short utterances that could accompany the facial expressions and practise them. For example:

"Urrrrgh! That's disgusting"! (grimacing)

"Ooooh! I can't stand the sight of blood"! (wincing)

c. Get everyone to make tight eyes ie. stiff and semi-closed. What effect does this have? What emotion does it suggest? What kinds of characters might have tight eyes? Now get everyone to make open eyes. Ask the same questions. Tight eyes might suggest evil, confusion, tiredness etc. Open eyes might suggest vulnerability, innocence, awe etc.

d. Working with a partner, learners see if they can express the emotions below with their eyes only. Their partner guesses which emotion is being expressed. To make it more challenging, students can cover up the lower half of their faces with a piece of paper.

furious   upset   excited   shy   exhausted   curious

Ask students to think of two more feelings for their partner to guess.

Eye contact:

e. Discuss in plenary why eye contact is important. On stage, it is essential you make genuine eye contact with your co-actors in order to provoke a spontaneous, natural and meaningful reaction as well as to convince your audience that the actor is "in the moment". Expressionless glassy eyes suggest that an actor is simply going through the motions and reciting his/her lines with no emotion. Occasionally, it is necessary for an actor to speak directly to the audience. With a small audience, making genuine eye contact does not pose too much of a problem but with large audiences it is more difficult, but nevertheless still possible to make people 'feel seen'.

f. Make groups of six but first work in pairs within that group. Think of a basic activity such as saying the alphabet, counting to or backwards from a hundred, talking about your life or saying the days of the week followed by the months of the year repeatedly. Perform the activity making 'genuine' eye contact throughout. Ask the 'audiences' if they 'felt seen'.

Now in their groups of six, one student performs the activity as though addressing the others. The 'audiences' should be seated with their right elbow resting on their right knee with the right arm upright. As the 'presenter' begins speaking, the audience members slowly lower their arm until 'genuine' eye contact is made. As soon as it is made, their arm goes back to the upright position. The presenters' objective is to ensure that nobody's arm is ever completely lowered. Audience members make a high-pitched 'beep beep' sound if their arm is completely lowered. The outcome should be that the presenters need to continually and randomly share their eye contact amongst the audience.

19. It's the way I walk

Time: 30 – 45 minutes

Preparation: None

Procedure: The aim of this series of exercises is to help our inexperienced actors look and feel natural, comfortable and less self-conscious when standing and walking on stage. People inexperienced in acting or making presentations are often unaware of the distracting effect shuffling their feet, standing with their hands in their pockets or playing with their hands can have on an audience. The objective is not to change the learners' own way of walking and standing but simply to make them more aware of their bodies should the need arise to modify their walk or posture etc for characterisation purposes.

Place a chair at the front of the room. Invite a volunteer out of the room for a few seconds so you can give him/her instructions. Tell your volunteer that s/he should enter the room and simply stand in front of the chair not saying a word. Let him/her do this for a maximum of 30 seconds. Thank the volunteer and then take a second person out of the room and instruct him/her to go back in and 'guard' the chair, ie. act as though s/he is protecting it from the others. Again, no speech is necessary. Warn against overacting. Let this go on for about 30 seconds.

Follow this up with a discussion about the differences between the two: what usually transpires is that the first person looked uncomfortable and self-conscious, probably fidgeting, shuffling feet or standing with hands in pockets. In other words, there was no *purpose* for him/her to be standing there. The second person clearly had a *purpose* or *task*, even though it might not have been immediately obvious to the audience. Explain to the group that even when they are not at the centre of the action, perhaps standing in the background saying nothing, they still need to maintain energy, concentration and motivation i.e. have a clear *purpose* in mind. Why are they there? Are they watching and listening to what is going on? Should they be reacting?

Interestingly, inexperienced actors don't feel comfortable standing with their arms by their sides. They tend to play with their hands or put them in their pockets, which can be distracting for the audience.

Now explain to the group that you are going to concentrate on movement. Explain that when people walk, they tend to lead with a particular part of their body, e.g. their knees or chest. This can be quite a revelation to some! Line them up at one end of the room and ask each learner to walk the length of the space as naturally as possible. The objective for you and them is to ascertain which part of their body they lead with. It is not always obvious but should be for most.

Once you have established where each learner walks from, ask them to mill around the space at normal speed. After 30 seconds, ask them to speed up. Then after another 30 seconds, they revert to normal speed.

Now as they are moving at normal speed, ask them to exaggerate the movement of the part of the body they lead with ie. if they walk from their knees, they imagine a piece of string is attached to the knees and is pulling them along. Experiment by slowing and speeding up the pace.

Now in turn, call out various parts of the body which the learners must walk from. Remind them that they should imagine a piece of string is attached to the body part called out and they are being pulled along by it. Examples are: chest; right leg; both knees; left shoulder; both hips; nose; forehead. Students should exaggerate the walk.

Now go through this sequence again but they should not exaggerate. They should begin to realise that they are developing different ways of walking that might give them ideas for their own characters in the play.

End with a game of Tag. The person who is the chaser must create an unusual way of walking which everyone else copies. When someone is caught, s/he creates a completely different and bizarre way of walking for everyone to copy.

20. Image acting

Time: The whole rehearsal period

Preparation: None

Procedure: A good actor is a keen observer of life, people and everyday behaviour. Stanislavski (see Exercise 14) encouraged actors to bring their observations to their characterisations and termed the technique Image Acting. Occasionally for *general purposes only*, it is possible to base your whole character on either someone you know (friend, acquaintance, colleague or relative) or on a fictional character you have seen on stage or screen. More often than not though, actors tend to 'borrow' individual characteristics or mannerisms such as the way a person stands, walks or sits. The latter is preferable because total imitation lacks originality and personal creativity.

Give your learners an Observation Sheet, such as the one below.

Observation sheet

While you are developing your character, it can be useful to observe people in the street, in a department store, in a café, in a dentist's waiting room, in a train etc so that you might 'borrow' certain characteristics or mannerisms for your own character. Use the list below as a guideline and be prepared to share your findings at various rehearsals with the rest of the group. Naturally, you will have to demonstrate what you have observed.

Voice qualities:

e.g. speaking with a husky or high-pitched voice, speaking when drunk, using your voice to exert a high status over someone, speaking with an impediment, e.g. a lisp or stammer

Mannerisms and habits:

e.g. running your hands through your hair, looking over your glasses, picking your teeth, constantly sniffing or biting your nails.

Walking:

e.g. how do old/very young/fat/very tall people walk? and people with a disabiiity or limp? and people in authority?

Everyday activities:

e.g. how do various people hold a cup of coffee, stand, sit, get out of a chair or smoke?

Proxemics:

e.g. Observe the distance people keep when they are having a conversation, sitting on a train or in a doctor's waiting room.

---

21. Stage directions

Time: 15 minutes

Preparation: Draw the diagram opposite on the whiteboard or put it on an overhead transparency.

Procedure:

    a. Space students out on stage or in your rehearsal area making sure they can all see the diagram.

    b. Give them random instructions which they should follow, such as:

       "Take two paces downstage right"

       "Move one pace upstage centre"

       "Take three paces centre left"

       "Take four steps downstage centre"

       "Move one step upstage centre"

       "Take three paces downstage left"

       "Take one pace downstage centre"

       "Move five steps upstage right"

       "Move two paces centre right"

    c. Remove the diagram from the whiteboard (in case any are tempted to peek) and ask learners to go back to their original positions in the space. Ask them to shut their eyes as you give a *new* set of instructions which they follow.

You'll soon see who hasn't learnt the terminology!

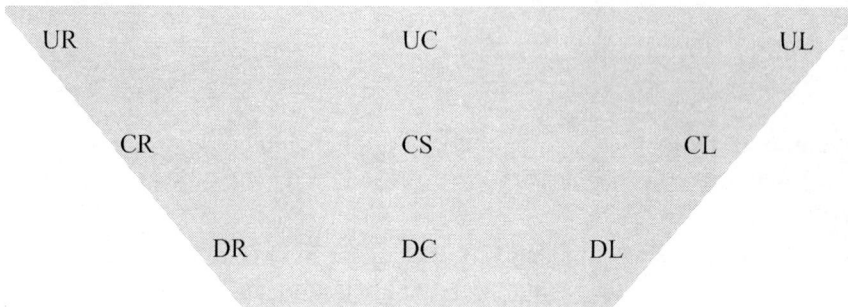

UR	UC	UL
CR	CS	CL
DR	DC	DL

A U D I E N C E

UR = Upstage Right

UC = Upstage Centre

UL = Upstage Left

CR = Centre Right

CS = Centre Stage

CL = Centre Left

DR = Downstage Right

DC = Downstage Centre

DL = Downstage Left

Comments: Towards the audience is called 'downstage' because stages used to be raked, ie. slope towards the audience.

As well as providing our learners with fresh specialist vocabulary, which is often greeted with enthusiasm, using these stage directions during rehearsal can make proceedings move along more quickly and smoothly.

Recommended Resources

Websites

Guide to selecting plays

www.samuelfrench-london.co.uk

Tongue twisters

www.geocities.com/Athens/8136/tonguetwisters

Rhymes

www.bbc.co.uk/cbeebies/tweenies/songtime/songs/t/thegrandoldduke of yorkshtml

Taglines

www.imdb.co.uk

Journals

English teaching Professional **www.etprofessional.com**

Modern English Teacher **www.onlineMET.com**

Glossary

Below is a list of vocabulary related to acting and the theatre. I have only selected the words and expressions that are useful to students during rehearsal and performance. Once they enter into this other world of theatre, students are keen to learn the meta-language that goes with it.

A

to ad lib
> impromptu unscripted speech or action usually because an actor has forgotten his/her *lines*

an audition (to hold an audition)
> when actors read for the Director hoping to be cast in the play

> **to audition (for s.b)**
> to read for a *character* you would like to play

B

backstage crew
> non-actors in charge of sound, lighting, prompting or scene shifting

blackout
> complete darkness *onstage*

to block a scene
> determine where the actors stand or move *onstage*

C

the cast
the actors

a character
person in the play

to be in character / to come out of character

to corpse
inadvertent laughter caused by nervousness

costume (to wear/be in costume)
a *character's* clothes

to have a c. c.
when a *character* has to change clothes between scenes

cue
the line/action before *your* line

to give someone their cue
to feed someone the line before *their* line

to pick up your c. more quickly
to react more naturally and quickly to lines

the curtain call
when the *cast* take their bow at the end of the performance

D

diaphragm
hence *diaphragmatic breathing*
the muscle separating the lungs from the abdomen

a dress rehearsal
the final rehearsal which should be treated as a performance ie. full
costume, sound etc and no interruptions

E

an entrance/exit
>   when an actor comes on or goes *offstage*

F

Front of House
>   non-actors in charge of distributing programmes and showing the
>   audience to their seats

a full house
>   every seat in the theatre is taken

I

to improvise
>   to act out a scene with little or no preparation

an interval
>   usually a 20-minute break between Acts. There is usually no need for an
>   interval if you are staging a one-act play

L

a lead/principal role

>   **to play a *lead/principal role***
>   one of the main characters in a play

lines

>   **to learn your l.**
>   the words a character speaks

a line run-through
to go through the play without acting. This is best done quickly with everyone seated in a circle

M

to mask/block s.b
to stand in front of another actor preventing the audience from seeing him/her. To be avoided

O

on/offstage

to be *on/offstage*

to say s.t *on/offstage*

to walk *on/offstage*
on the stage seen by the audience or in the wings or behind the stage not in view of the audience

opening night
the first performance

to overact
to act in an exaggerated and unnatural way

P

a prompt
the person who sits in the wings and follows the dialogue. If an actor forgets a line, the prompt supplies it

to prompt s.b
> to supply an actor with his/her line if it is forgotten

a prop
> short for 'properties'. Smaller objects used by actors on stage

R

to rehearse
> to practise before the performance

S

a scene change
> when furniture *onstage* is removed or replaced between scenes

a scene shifter
> the person who takes furniture *on/offstage* between scenes. Usually done by a non-actor but actors can do it if convenient

a script
> short for manuscript, the text of the play used in rehearsal

sightlines
> the view from the audience's perspective. You should aim to make sure actors can be seen from any angle

W

wings

to wait in the w.
> the areas left and right of the stage where actors wait to go on

Useful Phrases

"Books down"
when you expect your actors to have learnt their *lines*

"Break a leg"
it's considered unlucky to say "Good luck" so we say this instead!

"Go from the top"
start from the beginning of a scene/the play (again)

"I've got a big/small part in the play"
have a major/minor role in the play

"Kill the lights/sound"
turn the lights or sound off immediately. They can also be faded up or down

"Strike the set"
completely clear the stage of furniture and props, usually used after the final performance

"What part do you play"?
"What character are you"?

"What's your motivation"?
"Why does your character say/do that?"

Bibliography

Drama in ELT

Almond, M (2004), **English Teaching Essentials: Drama**, *English Teaching Professional*, Issue 35

Almond, M, **Curtain Up**, *English Teaching Professional,* Issue 22, 2002, www.etprofessional.com

Almond, M, **Bridging the Gap: Raising Cultural Awareness and Developing Communicative Skills Through Drama** (Hong Kong Institute of Education, 2001)

Butterfield, T **Drama Through Language Through Drama** (Kemble Press, 1989)

Dornyei, Z and Thurrell, S, **Strategic Competence and How to Teach it**, ELTJ 45/1, 1991

Dornyei, Z and Thurrell, S, **Conversations and Dialogues in Action** (Prentice Hall, 1992)

Dougill, J **Drama Activities for Language Learning** (Macmillan, 1987)

Hayes, S **Drama as a Second Language** (National Extension College Trust, 1984)

Holden, S **Drama in Language Teaching** (Longman, 1981)

Maley, A and Duff, A **Drama Techniques in Language Learning** (CUP, 1978)

Wessels, C, **From Improvisation to Publication**, ELTJ 45/3, 1991

Wessels, C, **Drama** (OUP, 1987)

Acting and Improvisation Theory and Practice

Benedetti, J **Stanislavski – an introduction** (Methuen, 1989)

Benedetti, J **Stanislavski and the Actor** (Methuen, 1998)

Fredman, R & Reade, I **Essential Guide to Making Theatre** (Hodder and Stoughton, 1996)

Gould, M **The Complete GCSE Drama Course** (Folens, 2000)

Johnston, K **Impro** (Methuen, 1979)

Johnston, K **Impro for Storytellers** (Routledge 1999)

Stanislavski, C S **Building a Character** (New York Theatre Arts Books, 1949)

Stanislavski, C S **Creating a Role** (New York Theatre Arts Books, 1963)

Tauber, R T & Mester, C S **Acting Lessons for Teachers** (Praeger, 1994)

Voice Work

Berry, C **Voice and the Actor** (Virgin, 2000)

Berry, C **Your Voice and How to Use It** (Virgin 1994)

Maley, A **The Language Teacher's Voice** (Macmillan Heinemann, 2000)

Parkin, K **Ideal Voice and Speech Training** (Samuel French, 1969)

Rodgers, J **The Complete Voice and Speech Workout, Applause** (Applause, 2002)

Drama Games

Boal, A **Games for Actors and Non-Actors** (Routledge, 1992)

Boyd, N L **Handbook of Recreational Games** (Dover Publications, 1973)

Cassady, M **Acting Games** (Meriwether Publishing, 1993)

Novelly, M **Theatre Games for Young Performers** (Meriweather Publishing, 1985)

Poulter, C **Playing The Game** (Macmillan, 1987)

Theodorou, M **Ideas That Work in Drama** (Stanley Thornes, 1990)

Drama as a mainstream subject: Theory and Practice

Bolton, G **Drama as Education** (Longman, 1984)

Heathcote, D **Collected Writings on Education and Drama** (Hutchinson, 1984)

Neelands, J **Beginning Drama 11 – 14** (David Fulton Publishers, 1998)

Watkins, B **Drama and Education** (Batsford, 1981)

Way, B **Development Through Drama** (Longman, 1967)

Winston, J and Tandy, M **Beginning Drama 4 – 11** (David Fulton Publishers, 2001)

Sources for Plays

Samuel French's Guide to Selecting Plays, available from 52 Fitzroy Street, London, W1P 6JR or www.samuelfrench-london.co.uk or 020 7387 9373 (+44 20 7387 9373 outside the UK)

Shackleton, M **Double Act: Ten One-Act Plays on Five Themes** Edward Arnold

Index